LOGICAL THINKING PUZZLES

For Alison, Melanie, Jim and Tom

Published in 2021 by Welbeck,
an imprint of Welbeck Non-Fiction Limited,
part of Welbeck Publishing Group
20 Mortimer Street, London W1T 3JW

First published by Eddison Sadd Editions in 2009

A CIP catalogue record for this book is available from the British Library

ISBN 978-1-78739-727-9

10 9 8 7 6 5 4 3 2 1

Printed in China

LOGICAL THINKING PUZZLES

BRAIN-TRAINING PUZZLES TO IMPROVE ANALYSIS AND DECISION-MAKING

CHARLES PHILLIPS

CONTENTS

INTRODUCTION

HOW TO THINK LOGICALLY

Have you ever looked back on something you've done and thought, "Why did I ever think that was a good idea?" Or do you listen to arguments and counter-arguments in news analysis and wonder, " Without becoming an expert in this field, how can I judge who is more likely to be right?" Logical thinking gives you the tools to make good choices, to distinguish between badly reasoned and soundly reasoned arguments. When you understand and apply a few basic rules of logical analysis, you learn to think more clearly. And you safeguard your independence of mind.

A THINKER'S JOURNEY

Logical thinkers make a journey from an initial statement called a premise through one or more steps in a linked chain to a final statement called the conclusion. In a logical argument, all the steps in the sequence are sound. If the initial premise is true, the final conclusion must be true. But in an illogical argument, the steps in the journey do not necessarily follow one after the other. Even if the premise is true, the conclusion may be false.

LOGICAL ALGEBRA

The following is an example of a logical argument: All Xs are Y; all Ys are Z; therefore all Xs are Z – "All Labradors are dogs; all dogs are mammals; therefore all Labradors are mammals." A slightly different formulation often seems logical at first sight, but it is not: All Xs are Y: Z is a Y; therefore Z is an X – "All cats are mammals; the blue whale is a mammal; therefore the blue whale is a cat."

The conclusion is plainly wrong in this example, but in abstract political or religious arguments, this kind of flawed logic sometimes appears, and it can be much more difficult to be sure of right and wrong. Then, an ability to recognize illogical reasoning helps you maintain clarity.

BEWARE FALSE PREMISES

You can present a perfectly logical argument, but if the premise is false, then the conclusion will be false too. Consider this: "Children are always truthful; Tom is a child; therefore Tom never lies." This statement may be impeccable in terms of the logic used to reach it, but it is based on a questionable premise.

DEDUCTIVE AND INDUCTIVE

There are two main types of logical argument. A deductive argument is one in which the premise completely supports the conclusion; an inductive argument is one in which the premise supports the conclusion, but not completely. In the real world we often have to rely on inductive logic. We cannot always find premises that are 100 per cent true, so we have to rely on what we can justifiably hold to be correct. Then, if we make sure we use logic in our argument, we will reach a conclusion that is probably true.

LOGIC AND EMOTIONS

One key reason why we make bad decisions is that we allow emotions to interfere with our thinking. Sometimes we have an emotional investment in reaching a particular conclusion – then we are usually very good at persuading ourselves that the choice we want to make is in fact the right one.

This could be a finely balanced problem, such as whether to try to buy a house or carry on renting, or whether to invest your savings in a friend's business. If you afterwards regret the choice, you probably wonder " Why couldn't I have thought more clearly about the pros and cons?" Logical thinking is invaluable in these situations. Using the basics of logic, you can examine your options and your goals, and judge whether doing what you want to do is really in your best interests.

LOGIC AND CREATIVITY

Logic is not enough on its own. Being logical is a good thinking strategy, but it is not the only goal. To think really well you usually need to combine logic with creativity and intuition.

BE POSITIVE

A crucial first step in improving any type of thinking is to be positive. We concentrate and perform much better when we are feeling good about ourselves. So, with all this in mind, let's get started!

INTRODUCTION

THE PUZZLES IN THIS BOOK

There are three levels of puzzles, each with a "time to beat" deadline. These deadlines apply a little pressure – we often think better when we have goals such as time constraints. But don't worry – if you find you take longer than the "ideal" time, relax. Some puzzles have another similar version later in the book to give you even more practice.

Look out for puzzles marked Time Plus. You'll need a bit longer to complete these – not because they are more difficult as problems but because there's more work to do before you can solve them. Where we feel you might need some help, a tip has been provided, and there are Notes and Scribbles pages later on for note-making and scribbling! Also towards the end of the book, the Challenge is designed to give your newly acquired logical-thinking skills a good, solid workout. This has a suggested time limit of 10–15 minutes to give you a chance to consider and reconsider the challenge, to plot the links in a logical chain of thought, perhaps make a few notes in the margin provided.

Don't rush. Take as long as you want if faced with a particularly challenging problem – the important thing is to try to think in the way outlined. You'll find as your new logical-thinking skills develop that you quickly see a beneficial effect at work or when studying, and also in other areas of your life – you'll be able to identify bad or lazy arguments and show that you can think clearly, quickly and creatively.

PUZZLE GRADING	TIME TO BEAT
EASY = WARM-UP	1–3 MINUTES
MEDIUM = WORKOUT	4–6 MINUTES
DIFFICULT = WORK HARDER	7–8 MINUTES
TIME-PLUS PUZZLES	8+ MINUTES
THE CHALLENGE	10–15 MINUTES

50 PUZZLES FOR LOGICAL THINKING

REMEMBER. Concentrate! Look closely. Examine your own reasoning. Equip your mind to think **LOGICALLY**

EASY PUZZLES

FOR LOGICAL THINKING

WARM-UP

1-3 MINUTES

The puzzles in this first section of the book give your logical-thinking skills a warm-up. They offer a chance to practise looking very closely and interpreting what you see. They'll develop your visual logic and your ability to draw inferences from information. And they are designed to be fun! Approach these puzzles in a positive frame of mind. Keep on your toes – look as closely as you can, read carefully. Make sure you understand what you're being asked to do. Go back to check. But don't be afraid to make mistakes because (as in other fields of life) you can learn plenty from going wrong.

PUZZLE 1

MR MOTHADA'S NUMBER PYRAMID

As a warm-up for the students in his secondary school computing class, Mr Mothada devises a number pyramid, shown below, to test logic and mental maths. Except in the bottom row, every brick contains a number that is the sum of the two numbers below it, so that F = A + B and so on. Can you work out all the missing numbers?

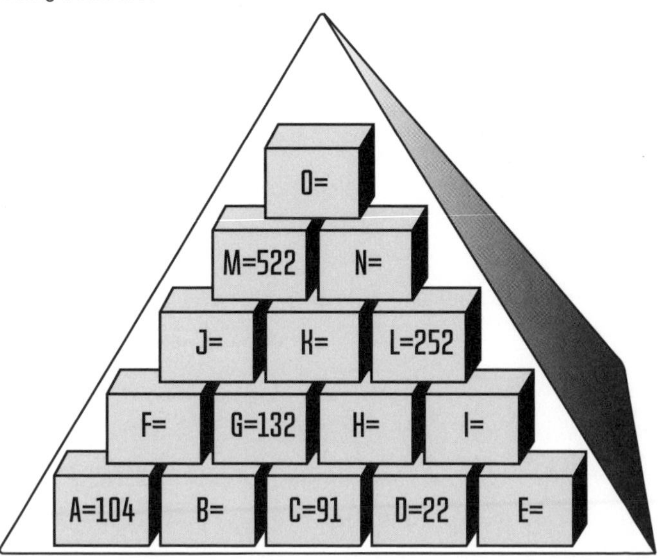

Start with H, and you'll soon have I and E. Mental maths is good exercise in the consistent use of reasoning that is so important for logical thinking.

1-3 MINUTES

PUZZLE 2

NUMBER BOARDS

Whichever summer job he takes, eternal student Gabriel always likes to bring a few logic and mathematics problems to it. When he is working at the ZigZag Hotel, he shifts the number boards used for hanging up room keys into the sequence shown below, then asks his colleague Marcus to work out the sequence. Can you help Marcus crack the code and replace the question marks with numbers?

10	3	6	7	?
1	?	5	4	9

Would it be odd if the even numbers made a sequence?

1-3 MINUTES

PUZZLE 3

DREW'S DOMINO TABLE

Artist Drew makes a special table to display his dominoes on, following the outline below. Numbers are painted on the table as shown, and he asks his guest Scottie to position the 28 dominoes in the set over the numbers so they all fit. Can you help Scottie by drawing in the outlines of the dominoes on the artwork below? The tick box is provided to help you. Drew placed one domino to get Scottie on her way. The dominoes fit in vertically and horizontally, but not diagonally.

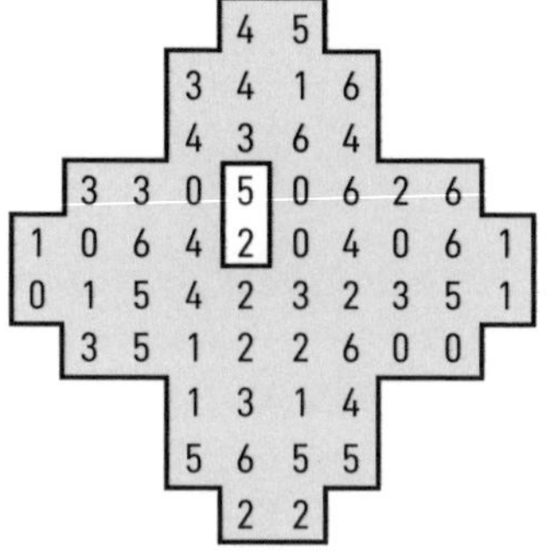

0-0	0-1	0-2	0-3	0-4	0-5	0-6

1-1	1-2	1-3	1-4	1-5	1-6	2-2

2-3	2-4	2-5	2-6	3-3	3-4	3-5
		✓				

3-6	4-4	4-5	4-6	5-5	5-6	6-6

Before you attempt this puzzle, photocopy the diagram or copy it onto a piece of paper – you can draw your answers in on the copy without marking the original, and can come back later to try the puzzle again, aiming to beat your time.

WARM-UP

TIME PLUS

PUZZLE 4
COLLEGE BICYCLE BELLS

Five student friends are at university, reading different subjects. They see one another regularly as they all cycle to their various lectures and always ping "Hello!" on their bicycle bells. Study the clues below to determine where each one has his or her lodgings, the subject he or she is taking at university, and the colour of his or her bicycle. Clues: 1. The student of History (not Hannah) lives in Saddle Street and has neither the silver nor the green bicycle. 2. Derek, who rides a startlingly bright orange bicycle, isn't studying History or Computing. 3. The student with lodgings in Wheel Way is neither Jimmy (who is studying Engineering) nor the student of Psychology (whose bicycle is neither green nor red). 4. The student with the silver bicycle is neither the one who lives in Handlebar Hill (who is studying Computing) nor Sharon, who lives in Chain Close.

		LODGINGS					STUDYING					BICYCLE				
		BELL BOULEVARD	CHAIN CLOSE	HANDLEBAR HILL	SADDLE STREET	WHEEL WAY	COMPUTING	ENGINEERING	HISTORY	LANGUAGES	PSYCHOLOGY	GREEN	ORANGE	PURPLE	RED	SILVER
STUDENT	DEREK															
	GEORGE															
	HANNAH															
	JIMMY															
	SHARON															
BICYCLE	GREEN															
	ORANGE															
	PURPLE															
	RED															
	SILVER															
STUDYING	COMPUTING															
	ENGINEERING															
	HISTORY															
	LANGUAGES															
	PSYCHOLOGY															

STUDENT	LODGINGS	STUDYING	BICYCLE

PUZZLE 5

GRIDBLOCK

Can you place all 12 of the blocks below into the grid? The numbers outside the grid refer to the number of consecutive black squares in each line or column, from left to right or top to bottom. Each block of black squares is separated from the others by at least one white square. For instance, 3, 2 could refer to a row with none, one or more white squares, then three black squares, at least one white square, two more black squares, followed by any number of white squares. Any piece may be rotated or flipped over. No piece may touch another piece, not even diagonally.

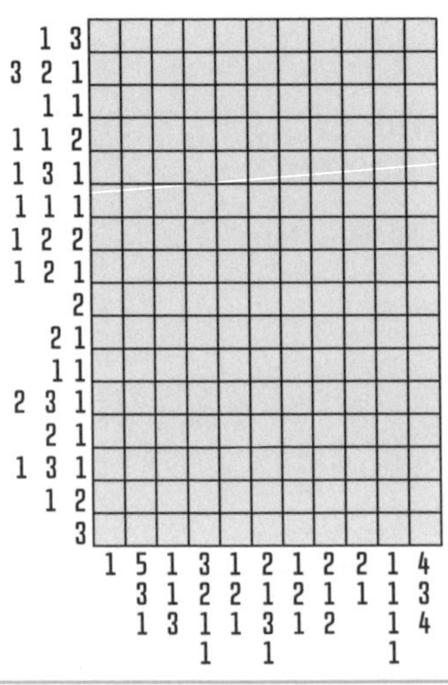

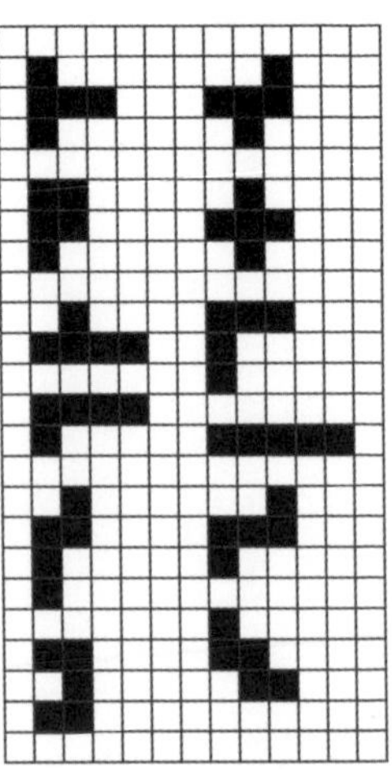

Play with the pieces. Visualize each in a number of forms.

WARM-UP

1-3 MINUTES

PUZZLE 6

"ONLY ONE OF THESE NOTES IS TRUTHFUL"

Perry comes home on his birthday to find that his brother has left four notes in the kitchen – one on the fridge, one on the cupboard door, one on the bread bin and one on the oven, plus there's a fifth on the front door that says: "Happy Birthday, Perry. Your present is in the kitchen. But only one of the notes you'll find there is truthful!" The four notes in the kitchen read as follows.

The fridge note says: "Your birthday present is in the cupboard or the oven!"
The cupboard note says: "Your birthday present is in the fridge or the bread bin!"
The oven note says: "Your birthday present is in here!"
The note on the bread bin says: "Your birthday present is not in here!"

Take a piece of paper and first try making notes of where the present *can't* be.

PUZZLE 7

THE "PATIENCE" OF HARRY STARRS

Child spy Harry Starrs is whiling away time on a stakeout and devises this version of the game "Patience" for his partner Hank. He draws 12 cards A–L, as shown, and asks Hank, "What is the face value and suit of each of the cards?"

Here are Harry's ground rules. Together the cards total 84. All 12 cards are of different values. (In the pack, the value of each card is as per its number, while Ace = 1, Jack = 11, Queen = 12 and King = 13.) No card is horizontally or vertically next to another of the same colour and there are four different suits in each horizontal row and three different suits in each vertical column. In addition:

1 The 6 is next to and above the 10, which is next to and above the 2 of Spades.
2 Card C has a value three lower than that of card F, which has a value three lower than that of card L, which has a higher value than that of card A.
3 The Ace of Hearts is next to and above a card with a value three higher than that of card H, which is of the same suit as card C.
4 The Jack of Diamonds is in the same horizontal row as a Club with a value two higher than that of card B.

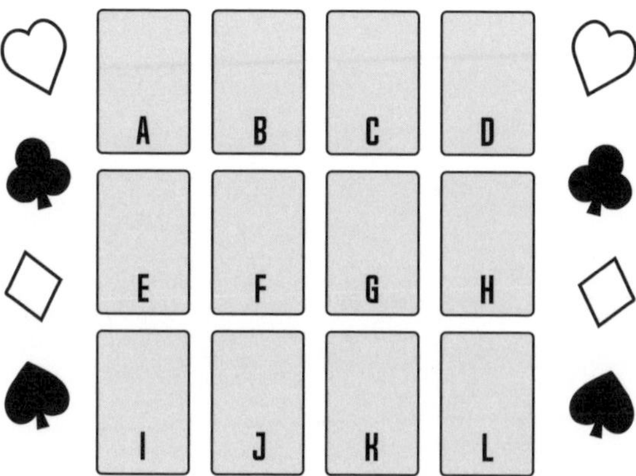

PUZZLE 8

CODE-CRACKING AT THE ZIGZAG

Eternal student Gabriel is still working in the ZigZag Hotel (see Puzzle 2). The guestbooks each have numbers on them, and Gabriel is playing around with them until business picks up. He arranges them as shown and then asks his colleague Seamus to rearrange them in a new sequence on the basis of the three clues below. Can you help Seamus crack the code?

Here are the clues provided by Gabriel: In the new sequence, the middle numbers add up to 5; the 4 is now to the left of but next to the 1; and the number on the far right is bigger than that on the far left.

Read the clues very carefully; try plotting the movements without writing anything down to exercise your short-term memory as well as developing your visual logic skills.

1-3 MINUTES

PUZZLE 9

TROPICAL FISH LIKE WARM WATER

I'm sure you remember Venn diagrams from maths class at school. Philosophy teacher Mr Alexis likes to use them to kickstart his students' visual logic and quick thinking before they move on to weightier matters. He prepares the diagram shown below, then asks his students, "Who can be fastest to work out which area of the diagram represents fish with blue tails and yellow fins that glow in the dark but don't live in cold water?" Angus is first with the right answer. What does Angus say?

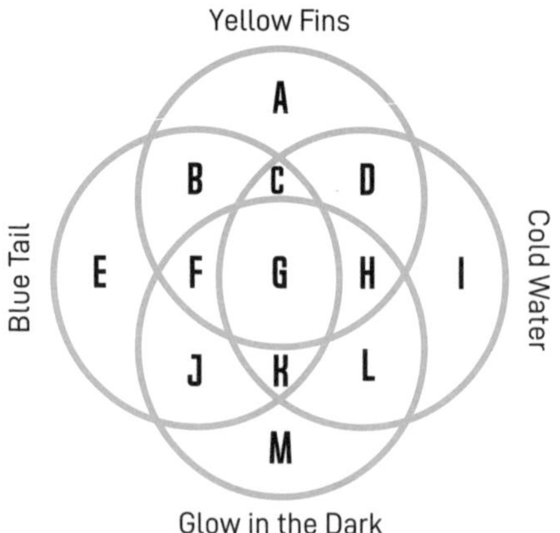

Dive in at the deep end, and be sure to read the question carefully, because it's easy to come to the wrong conclusion.

1-3 MINUTES

PUZZLE 10
MAKE A SUM

Student philosopher Carlo has found some coasters with the basic mathematical symbols for addition, subtraction, division and multiplication (+, −, ÷, x) and brings them to the "Sunset Vue" bar, where he is working for the summer. He arranges the six number coasters as shown below then asks his manager, Fabrizio, to make a sum by inserting the four symbols (+, −, ÷, x) between the numbers shown. He tells Fabrizio: "The mathematical symbols can be in any order, and only one has been used twice." Can you help Fabrizio find the correct answer?

6		3		5		7		4		8

=	13

You'll be doing well to solve this problem within the 3-minute target. Tick off the symbols you use as you go along. You may also want to note down possible sums as you go along, either in the book or on a piece of paper.

PUZZLE 11

NUMBER JIG

Fit the numbers into the grid. One 7-digit number has been filled in to get you started. Now find a six-digit number beginning with 4 (easy!) to continue, and so on.

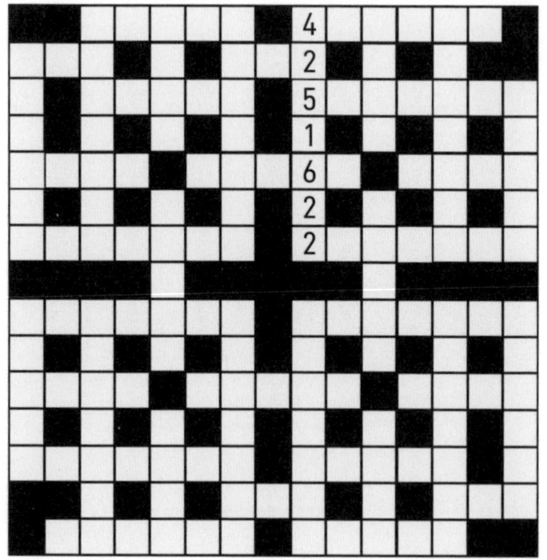

3 digits
187
652
765
963

4 digits
1908
2609
3313
4676
5212
6407
7024
8241

5 digits
19351
24007
30442
41693
50289
69734
72268
75913
87126
93775

6 digits
129194
272969
435432
501123

7 digits
1498016
1781640
2456733
3482667
~~4251622~~
4968451
5693211
5916894
6573079
7019855
7124356
8027294
9313857
9758036

1-3 MINUTES

PUZZLE 12

REBEKAH'S NUMBER WALK

For her party, maths whizz Rebekah chalked a number grid on her garden patio. She asked one of her guests, Ethan, to draw an unbroken line connecting all the dots horizontally or vertically at the corners of the squares on the grid. Some but not all of the boxes contain numbers telling you how many sides of that box must be drawn in. (If a box is empty, any number of its sides may be drawn in.)

3		3	3	3
1	2		2	1
	2			
2	3	3	2	2
2		2	2	3

Try starting in the top left-hand corner.

PUZZLE 13

SUDOKU

Can you fill in the empty squares so that each 3 x 3 block of nine squares, as well as each vertical column and horizontal row, contains the numbers 1 to 9 once and once only?

	6					7		
8		9		6		5		
2	4	5		1		8		
			5					4
	5	4				6	9	
3					6			
		7		5		1	2	6
		2		7		4		5
		1					7	

Try pencilling in the possible numbers that could fit in each square, column and row, and then eliminating the ones you don't need. The picture will gradually become clearer.

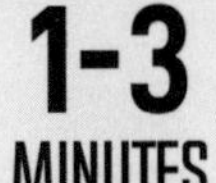

PUZZLE 14

NUMBERSEARCH

In this, our first Numbersearch, your task is to find one number in the grid, but first you have to calculate the sum of 55241 + 682290 – then look for the answer in the grid.

7	3	5	8	1	5	7	5	3	1	7	8
1	1	8	3	8	4	8	9	3	1	7	5
1	7	8	7	3	1	7	8	1	6	5	6
5	7	4	1	3	5	4	1	7	7	5	1
5	7	8	1	9	7	6	8	7	1	1	3
5	1	7	8	7	6	4	8	7	1	7	4
8	2	6	8	3	5	1	3	7	2	8	5
4	2	5	7	4	5	7	8	3	5	7	1
5	3	7	9	5	5	7	1	5	9	8	5
1	8	0	1	3	7	5	7	8	5	9	1
4	7	8	1	0	5	7	1	7	5	5	1
5	4	7	8	1	5	7	8	5	1	4	5

This is just like a wordsearch puzzle, except you're looking for one number only – and with the added twist that you have to work out the number you're looking for before you start.

1-3 MINUTES

PUZZLE 15

NUMBERZONE

Artist and mathematician Istvan devises a sequence of four sets of nine numbers for his nightclub installation "Numberzone". While he's setting it up, he tests his friend and helper Akos by asking him to choose from the five sets of numbers A–E to fill the fourth screen in the Numberzone. Which set should Akos choose?

7	3	8
1	2	1
5	9	6

3	2	4
2	7	4
8	5	7

3	1	2
6	7	4
4	6	9

?

A

6	2	1
4	3	7
2	9	8

B

6	4	7
4	5	2
3	5	6

C

2	6	2
3	5	3
8	4	7

D

3	2	1
8	4	7
1	8	7

E

2	2	8
3	3	1
6	9	5

Consider the vertical columns if you want to crack the code. Codes built on logic and code-breaking are a good test for those of us seeking to develop our powers of logical thinking.

WARM-UP

1-3 MINUTES

PUZZLE 16

MASYU

This is an example of a type of Japanese puzzle called the "Masyu". Squares on a grid contain white or blue circles, and your aim is to draw a single continuous line that passes through all the circles. These are the rules: the line must enter and leave each box in the centre of one of its four sides; at a blue circle, the line must turn left or right; at a white circle, the line must pass straight through; the line must pass straight through the box before and the box after a blue circle, without turning. The line must turn left or right in the box before and/or the box after a white circle. The line can turn left or right in an empty square. (Note that the line must not enter a box for a second time and must not cross over itself.)

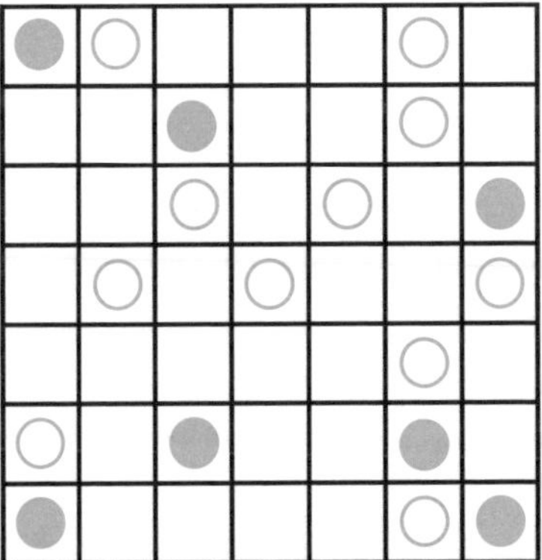

Use a pencil first time round, then try it again later, to give yourself a chance to take in all the rules fully.

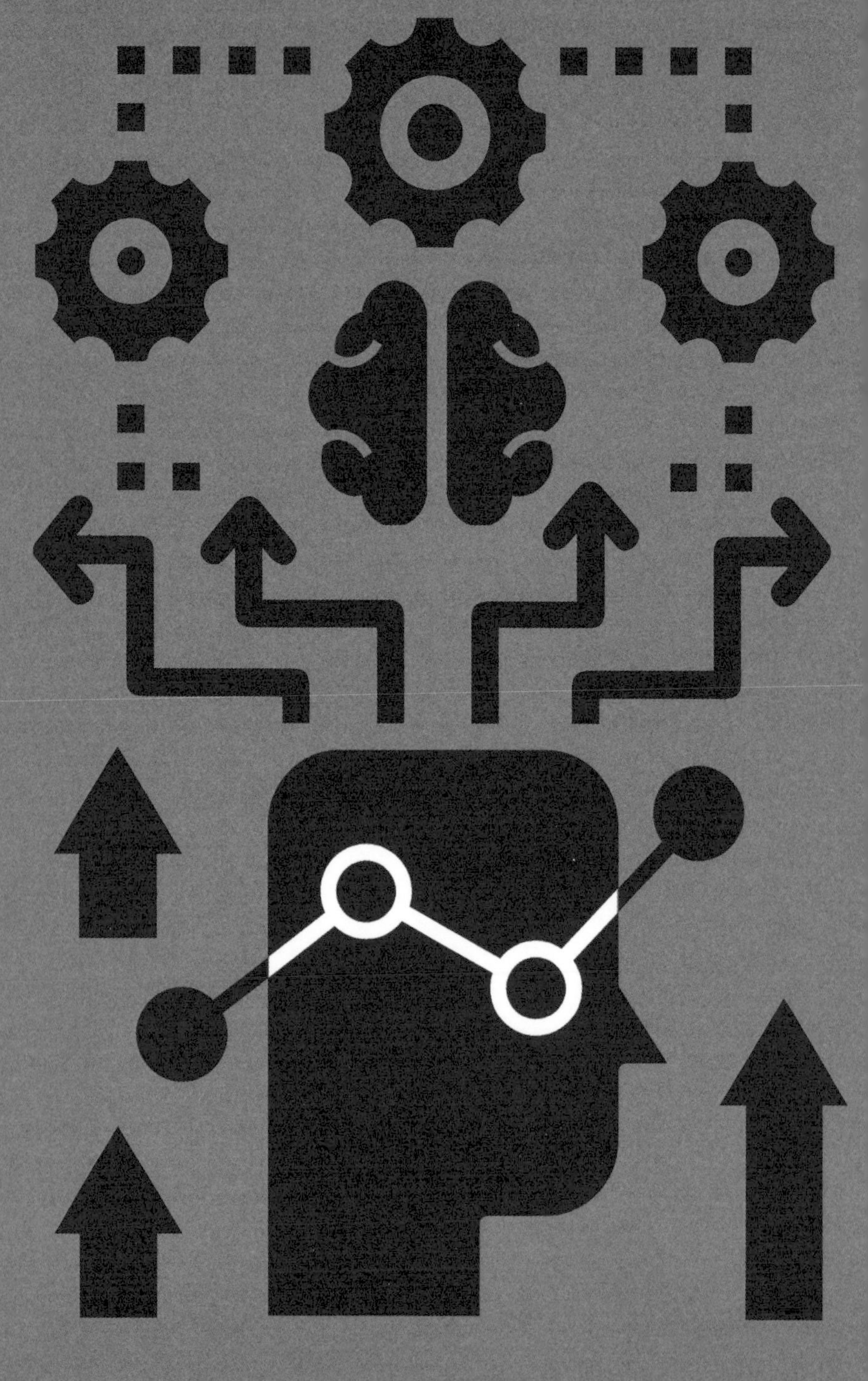

MEDIUM PUZZLES

FOR LOGICAL THINKING

WORKOUT

4-6 MINUTES

The second section of the book contains medium-difficulty puzzles designed to provide a more demanding workout for your developing powers of logical thinking. By now you're probably becoming familiar with the basics of logical thinking – reading figures and words with the closest attention, then tracing facts one to another, step by step, in a linked chain of inferences until you reach a rational conclusion. These skills are developed by solving numerical puzzles, finding your way through visual exercises and working our reasoning puzzles.

4-6 MINUTES

PUZZLE 17
CLYDE'S DOMINO TABLE

Drew has received so many plaudits for his domino table (see Puzzle 3) that he makes another one for his friend Clyde. Drew paints the numbers in a different position on the table from last time. He presents the table to Clyde and tells him that he has 6 minutes to lay out all the dominoes listed in the tick box below so the numbers match those on the table. If Clyde beats the 6-minute time limit, Drew says, he can have the table as a gift, otherwise he'll have to pay £100. Can you help Clyde get his table for free?

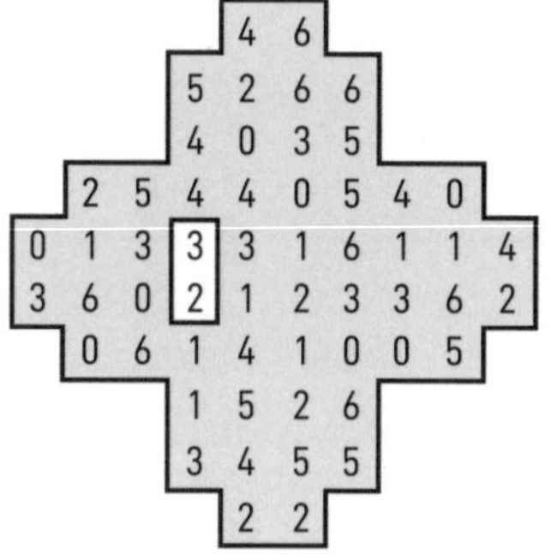

0-0	0-1	0-2	0-3	0-4	0-5	0-6

1-1	1-2	1-3	1-4	1-5	1-6	2-2

2-3	2-4	2-5	2-6	3-3	3-4	3-5
✓						

3-6	4-4	4-5	4-6	5-5	5-6	6-6

The double zero looks like an easy one to start with.

PUZZLE 18

FIVE FRIENDS AND THEIR PETS

Five friends each have a cat and a dog and a different number of fish. Discover the names of each child's cat and dog and the number of their fish.

1 The child who owns Ginger has twice as many fish as the boy who owns Rover.
2 Joey and Spot live in the same house, which isn't Josie's but may or may not be the house with three fewer fish than Josie's.
3 William has four more fish than Caroline.
4 The girl with two fish isn't Annie (whose dog is called Captain).
5 Patch lives with fewer fish than Sooty. Lenny is not owned by Annie.

	CAT					DOG					FISH				
	BOBBY	GINGER	JOEY	LENNY	SOOTY	BENJY	CAPTAIN	PATCH	ROVER	SPOT	2	3	4	6	7
ANNIE															
CAROLINE															
JOSIE															
MICHAEL															
WILLIAM															

CHILD	CAT	DOG	FISH

To work this one out, simply plot the information in the table and use your developing powers of reasoning to eliminate what is impossible – this will leave you with the truth.

4-6 MINUTES

PUZZLE 19

MIRROR SEQUENCE

Designer Piotr made these glass mirrors for the games room in a client's house. The client, Joshua, is a video-game maker with a playful character, and when he asks Piotr to rehang the mirrors he leaves his instructions in the form of a sequence of clues. Can you help Piotr work out the new sequence from these clues?

The white shapes are now adjacent.
The star has moved one place.
The square is now between the circle and the star.

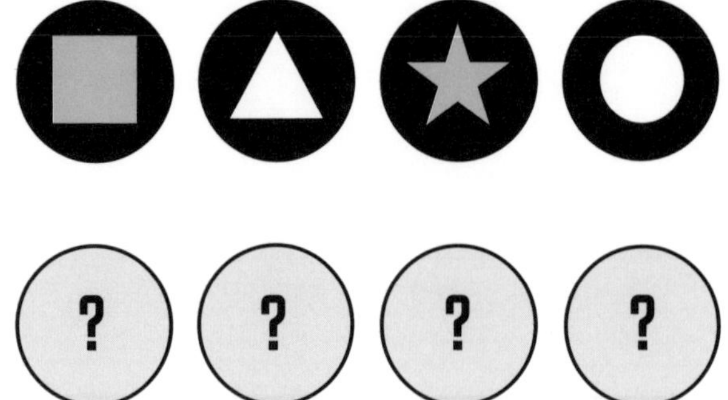

At first sight the clues may seem mutually incompatible, but read them again with your full attention, then plot the solution one step at a time.

PUZZLE 20

NUMBER SEQUENCE BOARD

Use numerical logic to crack the number sequence and complete the number board grid by replacing the question marks with the numbers that fit in the sequence.

10	11	9	10	8
?	5	6	4	9
11	?	6	8	7
13	12	?	13	15

Look for a sequence that starts from a number in the second row. The sequence may advance forward or backwards.

4-6 MINUTES

PUZZLE 21

BICYCLE BELLS, BASKETS, LIGHTS AND GEARS

Mr Alexis has drawn a new Venn diagram for his students (see Puzzle 9). This time he asks them, "Who can be first to work out which areas of this diagram represent: 1. bicycles with bells and baskets that don't have lights or gears; 2. bicycles with lights that don't have bells or baskets or gears; 3. bicycles with bells and lights but without baskets or gears?" Then he asks them, "My bicycle has a bell and gears and lights, but no basket. Where does it belong on the diagram?"

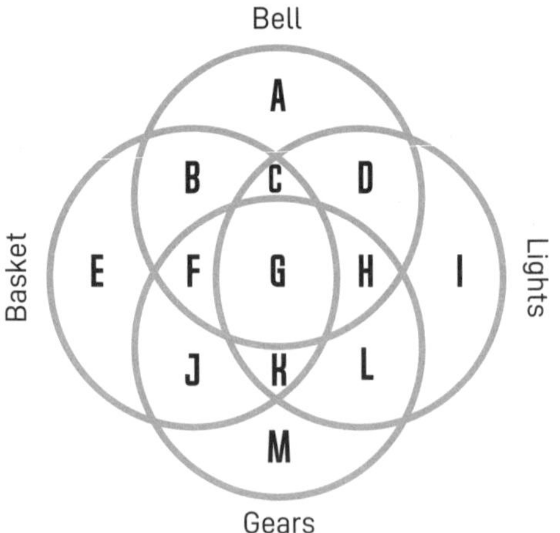

Keep the outline of the large circles of each grouping in mind as you read the information from the diagram.

4-6 MINUTES

PUZZLE 22

MAKE A SUM 2

Carlo has set up the number coasters on the bar of the Sunset Vue (see Puzzle 10) and is asking one of the delivery men, Angus, to create a working sum by placing the four maths signs (+, −, ÷, x) between the numbers shown. As before, Carlo says, "The math signs can be in any order, and one of them has been used twice." Can you help Angus?

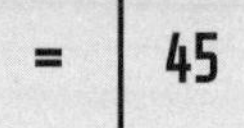

9		2		11		13		6		3

=	45

Try working backwards from the answer, 45. Multiply or divide by 3, add 3 to it, take 3 from it: see if this strategy helps you towards a likely figure. And remember – maths calculations are just like logical thinking – they must progress stage by stage to a conclusion that necessarily follows from the previous stage.

4-6 MINUTES

PUZZLE 23
ETHAN'S NUMBER WALK

Ethan devises a number walk to test Rebekah at her own game (see Puzzle 12). He chalks the number grid as shown below in the courtyard outside the students' common room. He asks Rebekah to connect all the adjacent dots at the corners of the squares on the grid with an unbroken line to form a number walk. "As in your game", he reminds Rebekah, "some but not all of the boxes contain numbers telling you how many sides of that box must be drawn in." (If a box is empty, any number of its sides may be drawn in.)

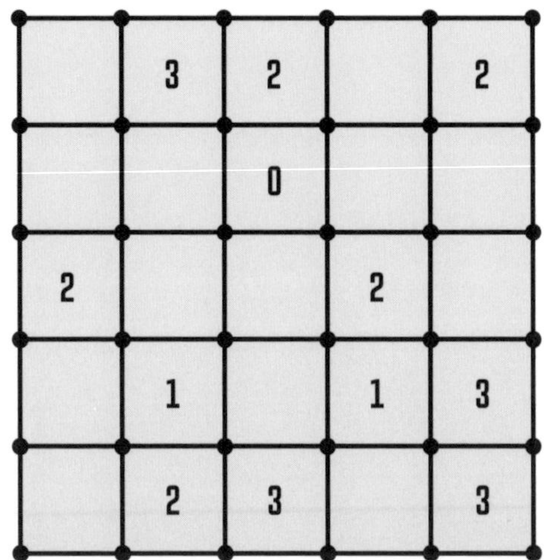

Remember: you have to join all the corner dots.

4-6 MINUTES

PUZZLE 24

MR MOTHADA'S NUMBER PYRAMID 2

After the success of his first number pyramid (see Puzzle 1), Mr. Mothada devises a second, slightly more challenging puzzle for his older students. As before, except in the bottom row, every brick in the pyramid contains a number that is the sum of the two numbers below it, so that F = A + B, etc. "Just work out the missing numbers!" he tells his groaning students.

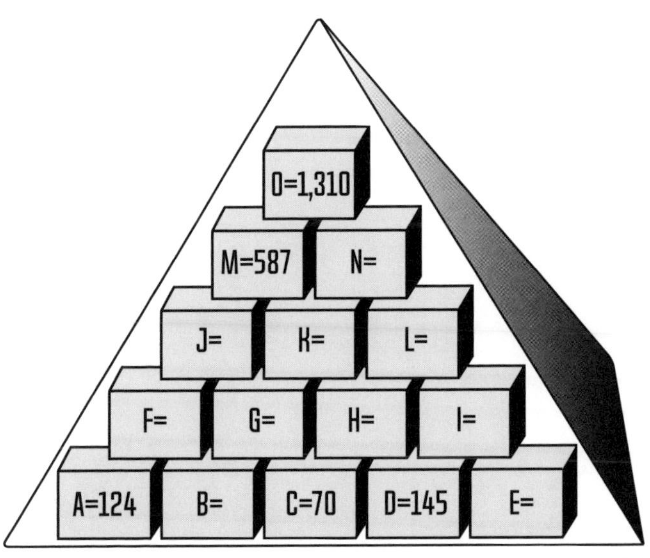

Your best bet is to start at the top.

PUZZLE 25

GRIDBLOCK 2

As in Gridblock 1 (Puzzle 5), the task is to place all 12 pieces into the grid. The numbers outside the grid refer to the number of consecutive black squares, from left to right or top to bottom; each block is separated from the others by at least one white square. For instance, 3, 2 could refer to a row with none, one or more white squares, then three black squares, at least one white square, two more black squares, followed by any number of white squares. Any piece may be rotated or flipped over, but no piece may touch another, not even diagonally.

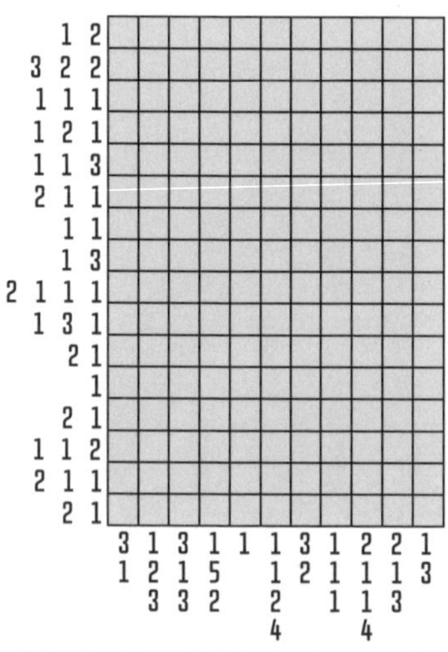

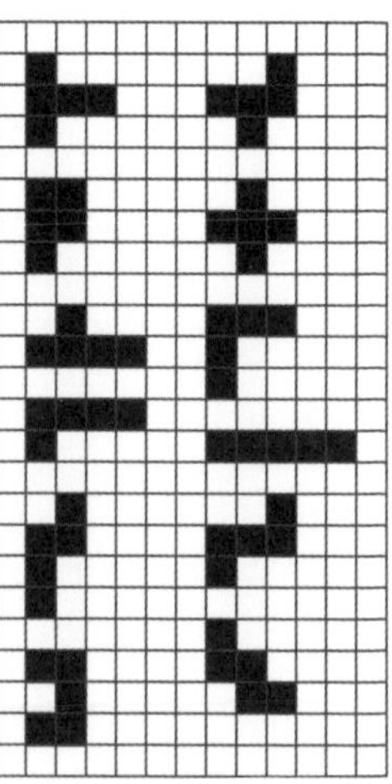

Have fun with the pieces as you visualize each in a number of forms.

4-6 MINUTES

PUZZLE 26

HARRY STARRS' SECOND STAKEOUT

Our child spy Harry Starrs (see Puzzle 7) has another long stakeout to endure, and his colleague Hank devises this card challenge to pass the time. He asks Harry, " What is the face value and suit of each of the cards shown below? Together they total 83. All 12 cards used are of different values. (In the pack, the value of each card is as per its number, while Ace = 1, Jack = 11, Queen = 12 and King = 13.) No card is horizontally or vertically next to another of the same colour and there are four different suits in each horizontal row and three different suits in each ve rtical column." In addition, he gives Harry these clues:

1 The King is directly next to and left of the 7, which is directly next to and below the 5 of Diamonds.
2 The 3 is directly next to and above the 9, which is directly next to and right of the Ace of Spades.
3 The 10 of diamonds is adjacent (either vertically or horizontally) to the Queen, which is of the same suit as the 4.
4 Card F has a value one higher than that of card J.
5 Card H is of the same suit as the 2. Can you help Harry identify the cards?

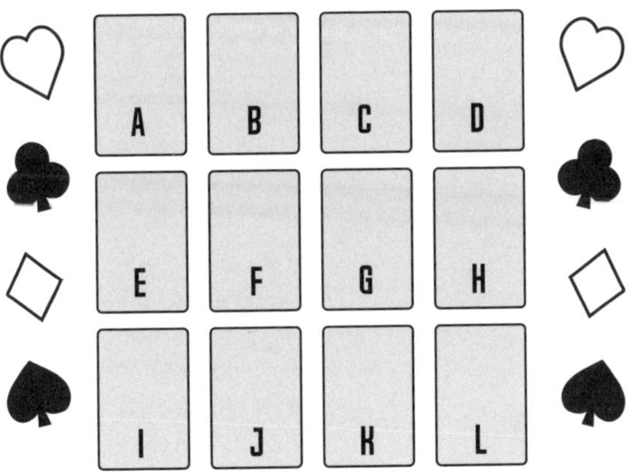

TIME PLUS

PUZZLE 27

NUMBERSEARCH 2

Can you find all of the answers to these clues hidden in the grid? The answers may run backwards as well as forward, in either a horizontal, vertical or diagonal direction, but must always be in a straight, uninterrupted line.

1 8917834 + 38947
2 2897,581 + 3902
3 771139 x 3
4 38928 + 387289
5 489289 x 838
6 932383892 – 778493
7 160 + 14 + 986
8 210 x 78
9 108 + 107 + 1031 + 8888
10 420 x 396

4	3	3	3	7	8	4	3	1	0	1	4
3	2	5	8	7	3	3	8	7	3	2	2
2	1	6	7	3	1	8	9	3	9	9	2
3	4	8	2	3	2	8	4	9	3	2	2
3	0	5	8	1	0	7	3	1	5	1	8
7	8	8	3	2	7	5	6	3	0	9	1
5	3	7	3	1	0	0	5	3	9	9	4
3	5	6	8	6	5	1	0	7	3	2	2
5	6	3	1	3	1	1	5	1	1	6	0
1	2	3	1	3	4	1	7	6	4	9	0
3	9	8	9	7	4	5	8	3	9	0	1
5	3	8	1	8	7	6	5	9	8	9	4

The added twist here is that you have to work out the numbers you're looking for before you start. Double-check your maths and your answers, otherwise you could be looking for some time!

WORKOUT

TIME PLUS

PUZZLE 28
DEL'S DELIVERIES

Del operates a delivery service, taking small consignments from one town to another for private customers and small businesses. Last week, he made five journeys. Can you discover not only from where and to where he travelled, but also his load on each day? The following clues contain all the information you'll need. 1. Del delivered several boxes of fruit for a small company the day before he went to Foursham, but later in the week than his journey from Eastering.
2. The cheese was transported earlier in the week than the shoes, which weren't collected in Northbrook. 3. Monday's trip wasn't to Threeton and Saturday's wasn't from Southford. 4. One journey was from Westbury to Oneford; and this took place either the day before or the day after the job that involved taking a consignment of stationery to Fivewood. 5. The trip to Twobury (not from Northbrook) took place two days later than that which started from Middleham.

		FROM					TO					LOAD				
		EASTERING	MIDDLEHAM	NORTHBROOK	SOUTHFORD	WESTBURY	FIVEWOOD	FOURSHAM	ONEFORD	THREETON	TWOBURY	BOOKS	CHEESE	FRUIT	SHOES	STATIONERY
DAY	MONDAY															
	TUESDAY															
	THURSDAY															
	FRIDAY															
	SATURDAY															
LOAD	BOOKS															
	CHEESE															
	FRUIT															
	SHOES															
	STATIONERY															
TO	FIVEWOOD															
	FOURSHAM															
	ONEFORD															
	THREETON															
	TWOBURY															

DAY	FROM	TO	LOAD

PUZZLE 29

SUDOKU 2

Fill in the empty squares so that each 3 x 3 block of nine, and each vertical and horizontal line contains the numbers 1 to 9, once and once only.

	2	7		8				
8	9	5		7		4		2
3			7	4	1			
		4				9		
			8	9	3			5
9		2		5		6	8	1
				1		5	2	

The numbers in the four corners of the large square add up to 25.

4-6
MINUTES

PUZZLE 30

NUMBER JIG 2

As with our previous Number Jig (see Puzzle 11), the task is to fit these numbers into the grid. One three-digit number has been filled in already to get you started. Perhaps the next step is to work out which of the seven-digit numbers whose second digit is 3 you should use?

3 digits
116
298
~~433~~
822

4 digits
1559
2810
3143
4292
5972
6703
8025
9432

5 digits
10165
29357
31274
48543
52927
64036
76480
83502
87219
95751

6 digits
342461
451839
629387
702276

7 digits
1380273
2013652
3820879
4034328
4757927
5173426
5223672
6367121
6742187
7262741
7631622
9134852
9196419
9253147

PUZZLE 31

OPEYEMI'S BOOKCASE

Here's another test of your close reading and your ability to draw inferences from information. On Monday to Saturday last week, Opeyemi bought a reference book each day. The books are in one of two sizes, either large or small, as represented in the diagram below. Can you discover the subject of each book Opeyemi bought, as well as the day on which he bought it? The following clues contain all the information you'll need. 1. Opeyemi bought the thesaurus two days before he bought the large book (not the atlas), which is next to and left of the book on the subject of weather patterns and predictions. 2. The book purchased on Wednesday is larger than (and isn't next to) the one that covers the subject of cookery, which was bought two days later than the atlas. 3. The book on trees was bought before a small book that is next to the volume dealing with the recognition of insects, which Opeyemi bought earlier in the week then the book on trees. 4. He bought one of the large books on Saturday.

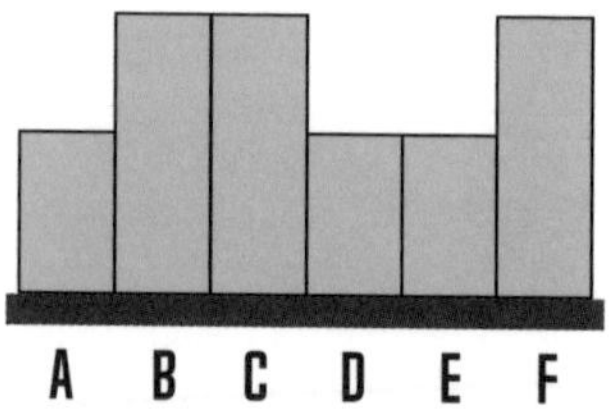

BOOK	SUBJECT	DAY PURCHASED

You might find it helps to make notes and draw a diagram, perhaps with linking arrows, when attempting this sort of logic puzzle.

PUZZLE 32

NUMBERSEARCH 3

As with our earlier Numbersearches (see Puzzles 14 and 27), your task is to find all the answers to the clues, hidden in the grid. The answers may run backwards as well as forward, in either a horizontal, vertical or diagonal direction, but always in a straight, uninterrupted line.

1 99 x 9 x 91
2 3827 + 4899620
3 387218 – 3896
4 88593 + 48970 + 874
5 848 x 827
6 992874 + 43903789
7 19929 – 83
8 84 x 12 x 108
9 9380 x 4890
10 3940 x 22

8	9	4	7	4	4	3	0	9	4	5	3
1	8	7	1	7	1	9	4	3	8	8	5
5	0	7	5	0	0	8	4	5	3	8	3
5	8	4	8	4	5	1	4	3	8	3	4
4	6	8	5	4	4	6	2	0	6	8	2
1	6	1	1	8	4	2	9	9	1	5	1
4	8	5	9	9	6	5	8	1	6	5	8
5	8	1	6	6	6	8	4	8	8	9	0
2	9	8	9	6	2	4	2	3	9	2	1
5	1	7	8	6	1	5	8	0	8	6	8
1	8	5	7	3	4	3	6	9	0	6	0
3	1	3	8	4	3	7	9	4	1	7	3

To get the most out of this puzzle, don't be reliant on a calculator! Brush up on your long multiplication. Do you think you could manage to do any of the sums in your head? It's worth trying because mental calculations are highly stimulating for brain cells.

WORKOUT

4-6 MINUTES

PUZZLE 33

NUMBERZONE 2

Artist and mathematician Istvan had designed another Numberzone installation (see Puzzle 16), a sequence of four sets of nine numbers. Now he's setting it up, and asks his friend Gitta to choose from the five sets of numbers A–E to fill the fourth screen in the Numberzone. Which set should Gitta choose?

15	81	57
49	98	63
36	54	18

9	33	48
28	84	14
63	12	39

24	15	63
21	56	91
78	42	84

?

18	9	36
35	63	9
45	39	21

A

77	30	45
84	28	21
57	12	27

B

3	30	53
70	42	56
48	69	3

C

6	66	27
98	21	35
14	51	24

D

21	75	54
77	14	42
33	6	42

E

Gitta divides her time into looking at the top, middle and bottom horizontal rows.

4-6
MINUTES

PUZZLE 34
VIKING LOGIC

Brunhilde, wife of Viking raider Bjorn Brighteye, is sorting out some boxes he has brought back from his latest pillaging trip. The three boxes, she has been told, are all wrongly labelled. One is marked "Skulls", one is labelled "Goblets" and one says it contains "Mixed Goblets and Skulls". Reaching in and taking just one item from one box, and without looking at the rest of the contents, Brunhilde is able to relabel all three boxes correctly. How?

Choose the box that will provide as much information as possible from a single object.

DIFFICULT PUZZLES

FOR LOGICAL THINKING

WORK HARDER

7-8 MINUTES

You'll have to work harder to solve the puzzles in this part of the book, which contains the most demanding of our exercises. Logical thinking is a meticulous, step-by-step mental process that demands precise observation, careful interpretation of the facts you are given and gradual progress along a path of reasoning, yet – especially in more challenging problems – you need to keep your creativity and intuition in play. If you feel stuck, put the book aside for a few minutes and come back to the problem. Try to imagine the question from a slightly different angle. Sometimes this enables you to make a breakthrough.

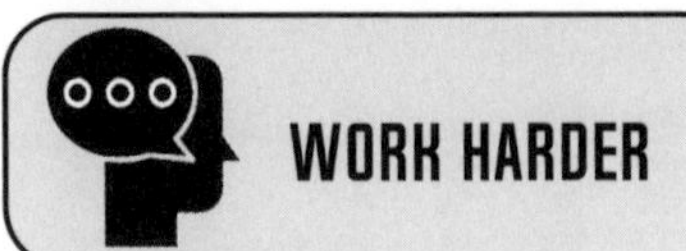

PUZZLE 35

DECORATOR DOUGAL'S BUSY WEEK

Dougal the Decorator has to paint the shopfronts of six businesses in the town centre. From the following clues, can you work out the order in which the shops can be found, and also which one is first on Dougal's list to paint? The following clues contain all the information you'll need. 1. The coffee shop is two buildings away from the first shop he is supposed to paint. 2. The crafts shop is three buildings from the grocer's. 3.The grocer's is the last stop in the street. 4. The first shop Dougal has to paint isn't the bakery. 5.The florist is three buildings from the coffee shop. 6. The bank is four buildings from the grocer's. 7. The florist is between the first shop he must paint and another business.

As with previous puzzles of this type, you'll probably benefit from drawing a diagram. Noting information in visual form is a good way of involving an additional part of your brain. Use as many parts of your brain as you can to stimulate thinking.

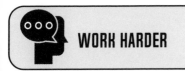

PUZZLE 36

HARRY STARRS' CARD STALL

Child spy Harry Starrs and his friend Hank have a real taste for their card game (see Puzzles 7 and 26). At their school fair they persuade the headmaster to let them set up a card stall for the game. Harry lays out the cards as shown below and asks customers, "What is the face value and suit of each of the cards shown?" This is what he tells them: "Together the cards total 82. All 12 cards used are of different values. In the pack, the value of each card is as per its number, while Ace = 1, Jack = 11, Queen = 12 and King = 13. No card is horizontally or vertically next to another of the same colour and there are four different suits in each horizontal row and three different suits in each vertical column." He also reveals that:

1. The Queen of Diamonds is next to and to the left of the 2, which is next to and below the 6, which is of a different suit to the 5.
2. The 4 of Clubs is next to and below the 7, which is next to and either to the left or to the right of a card that is next to and below the 10.
3. Card F has a value two higher than card I. The Jack of Spades is in the same horizontal row as the 3.
4. Card A is of the same suit as a card with a value two lower than that of card E, which is of the same suit as the card next to and left of the King.

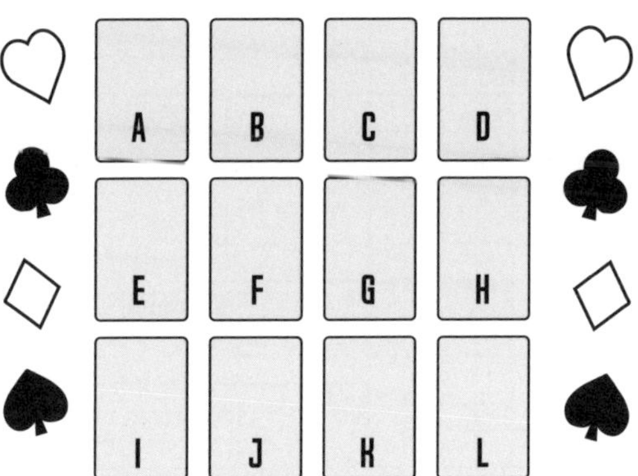

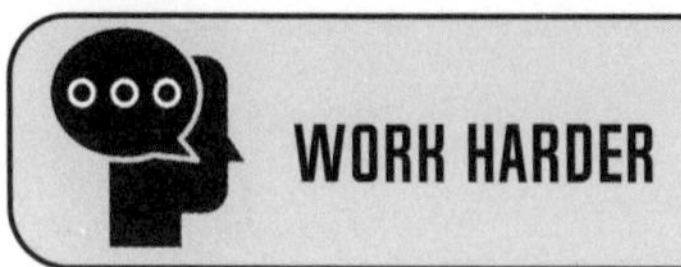

PUZZLE 37

TIMEKEEPING TROUBLES

My five sisters, Erica, Lynne, Doreen, Claire and Marian, were late for work this morning, due to reasons beyond their control. Can you work out where each works, how late she arrived and the reason? These clues contain all the information you'll need. 1. Erica wasn't exactly 40 minutes late for work. 2. Lynne works in a shop. The librarian (not Doreen or Erica) was exactly 30 minutes late for work. 3. The teacher (who was delayed from reaching the school by a violent hailstorm) was later for work than the woman held up by strong winds. 4. Claire was 20 minutes later for work than the woman whose alarm clock failed to work (who wasn't exactly 20 minutes late). However, Claire wasn't as late as the woman who works in the theatre. 5. The woman who blamed black ice was 10 minutes later than the woman who had to make a lengthy detour to avoid a fallen tree.

		WORKPLACE					REASON					MINUTES LATE				
		LIBRARY	OFFICE	SCHOOL	SHOP	THEATRE	ALARM CLOCK	BLACK ICE	FALLEN TREE	HAILSTORM	STRONG WINDS	20 MINUTES	30 MINUTES	40 MINUTES	50 MINUTES	60 MINUTES
NAME	CLAIRE															
	DOREEN															
	ERICA															
	LYNNE															
	MARIAN															
MINUTES LATE	20 MINUTES															
	30 MINUTES															
	40 MINUTES															
	50 MINUTES															
	60 MINUTES															
REASON	ALARM CLOCK															
	BLACK ICE															
	FALLEN TREE															
	HAILSTORM															
	STRONG WINDS															

NAME	WORKPLACE	REASON	MINS LATE

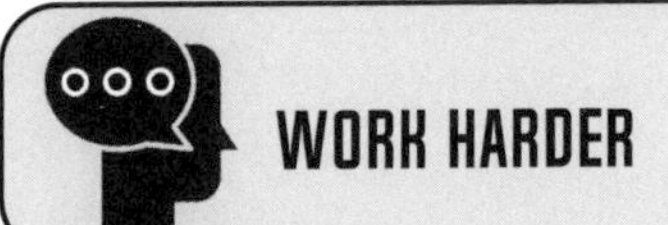

7-8 MINUTES

PUZZLE 38

ANDRE'S VIRTUAL DOMINO TABLE

Artist Drew sold the idea of his domino table (see Puzzles 3 and 17) to a games developer called Andre, who put it in his new video game "Logick". Players are told that a standard set of 28 dominoes has been laid out on the table. Their task is to draw in the edges of them all. Andre provides a tick box (below) as an aid and sets one domino in place to help the players – including you – on their way. Remember the pieces can be placed vertically or horizontally, but not diagonally.

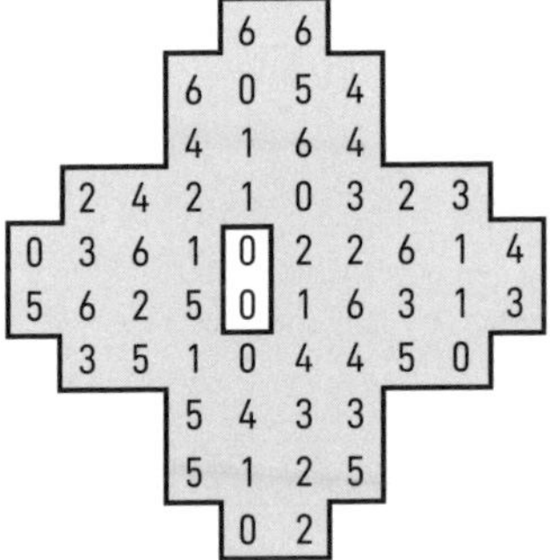

0-0	0-1	0-2	0-3	0-4	0-5	0-6
✓						

1-1	1-2	1-3	1-4	1-5	1-6	2-2

2-3	2-4	2-5	2-6	3-3	3-4	3-5

3-6	4-4	4-5	4-6	5-5	5-6	6-6

First identify which pieces have the fewest playing options.

PUZZLE 39
LETTER MATS

Andre's video game (Puzzle 38) called "Logick" centres around the Logica Hotel. Here, the table mats bear single large letters and are arranged in logical sequence. The letter mats shown below left have been rearranged. Can you work out how the mats could be arranged so that the following statements are all true:

1 The black hexagons are now touching one another.
2 F has moved and is now between two white hexagons.
3 Only one mat has not moved.
4 E is not next to C.

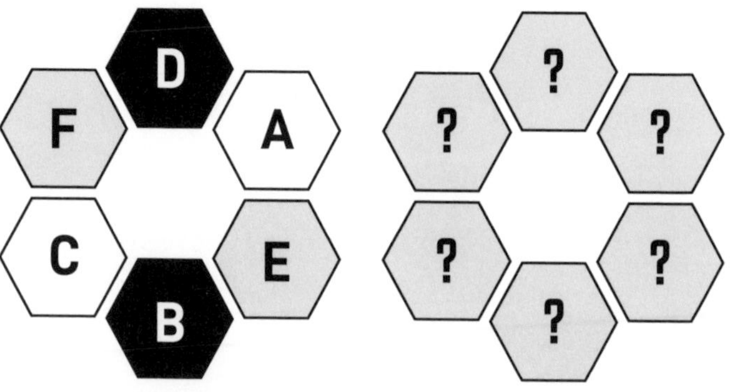

Remember – one of the mats is not moving. These puzzles, like games in which you have to make creative combinations within the constraints of rules, give your powers of logical thinking a real boost.

7-8
MINUTES

PUZZLE 40
JUMBLEHOURS

For a children's book about dreaming, Clarissa creates this crazy 24-hour clock with the numbers jumbled and without hands. The numbers are in sequence. Can you crack the number sequence and complete the circle by replacing the question marks with the numbers that fit in the sequence?

To break the code, treat each group of ascending numbers separately. Once you've done this puzzle, for a bonus challenge, can you come up with your own, different numbering sequence for arranging the numbers 1–24 around a clock in sequence?

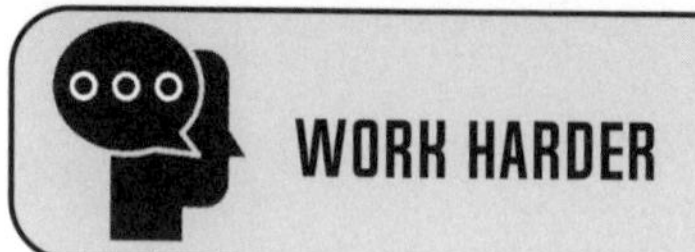

7-8
MINUTES

PUZZLE 41
CATS 'N' FISH 'N' FLEAS

Here's a third Venn diagram challenge devised by philosophy teacher Mr Alexis as a warm-up for his students (see Puzzles 9 and 21). He draws the diagram and writes his challenge on the whiteboard in the classroom. "Which areas of this diagram represent: 1. Black cats with white feet who like fish but don't have fleas; 2. Grey cats with white feet who have fleas but don't like fish; 3. Ginger cats without white feet who like fish and have fleas; 4. Cats with black fur and black feet who like fish but don't have fleas; 5. White-footed black cats who scratch at their fleas and gobble up fish; 6. Cats with black fur, white feet and fleas who refuse all foods except finely diced cooked chicken.

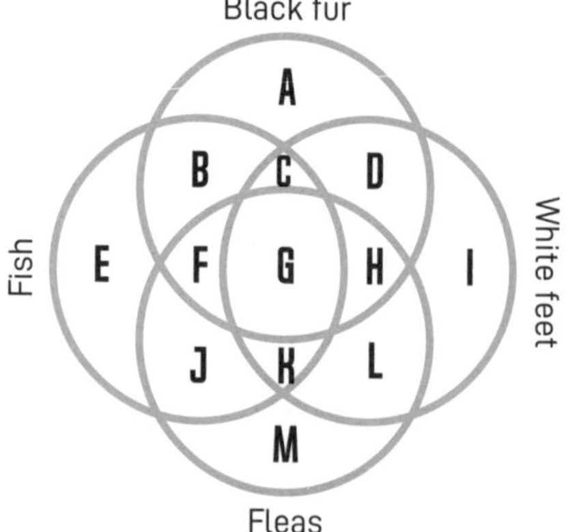

Concentrate on one clue at a time, If you have well-developed visual logic skills, you may find you're able to beat the time limit quite easily – well done! Others find this type of exercise more of a challenge, but don't worry if you're in this group – facility will come with practice!

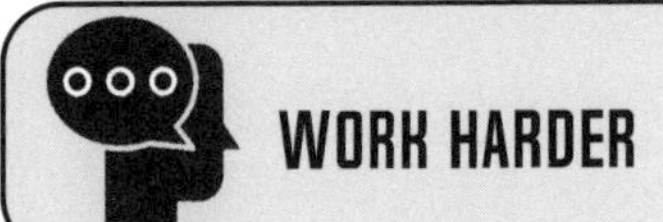

7-8 MINUTES

PUZZLE 42

MAKE A SUM 3

Business is booming in the "Sunset Vue" bar, where the customers really enjoy the "Make A Sum" game that barman and philosophy student Carlo sets up for them with the coasters (see Puzzles 10 and 22). Here's another chance to play. Carlo has laid out the number coasters as shown below and you have to make a working sum by inserting the four mathematical symbols (+, −, ÷, x) between the coasters. The symbols can be placed in any order, and one of them has been used twice.

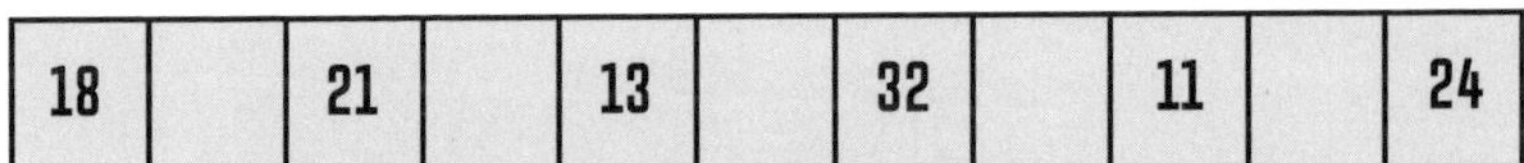

=	109

Carlo doesn't allow negative numbers, so the first symbol (between 18 and 21) has to be either a multiplication or an addition sign.

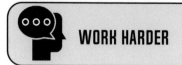

PUZZLE 43

GRIDBLOCK 3

Here's a third chance to test your powers of logic and visual dexterity with Gridblock (see Puzzles 5 and 25). Again, the task is to place all 12 pieces into the grid. Any piece may be rotated or flipped over, but none may touch another, not even diagonally. The numbers outside the grid refer to the number of consecutive black squares, from left to right or top to bottom; and each block is separated from the others by at least one white square. For instance, 3, 2 could refer to a row with none, one or more white squares, then three black squares, at least one white square, two more black squares, followed by any number of white squares.

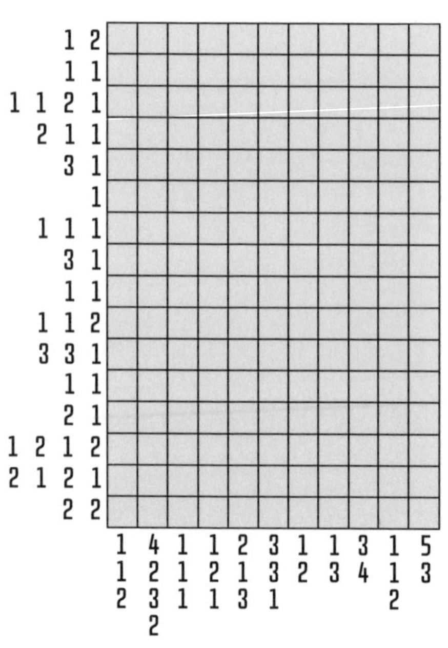

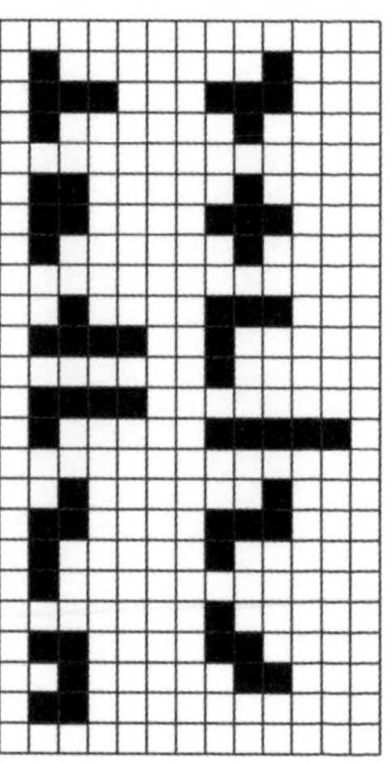

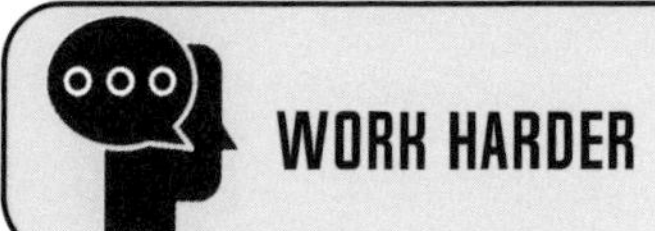

PUZZLE 44

PRIME NUMBER PATH

This is another puzzle from Andre's video game "Logick" (see Puzzles 38 and 39). A large room is paved with golden tiles, each of which has a number on it, as in the grid below. The task is to find your way from any square in the room's near side (the top row of the grid) to any square on the far side (the bottom row), passing only through prime numbers. (A prime number is any number such as 2 that can only be divided by itself and by 1.) You can move straight down and straight across – diagonal moves are not allowed.

4	30	68	63	49	27	9	19	87
18	22	14	89	97	2	15	37	81
17	44	66	53	4	11	79	73	9
29	12	77	5	24	49	77	33	57
71	23	36	7	25	59	31	83	23
16	45	18	71	67	23	62	15	61
2	61	19	14	8	18	44	12	79
11	10	83	59	29	47	13	17	97
43	62	99	21	32	33	46	75	55

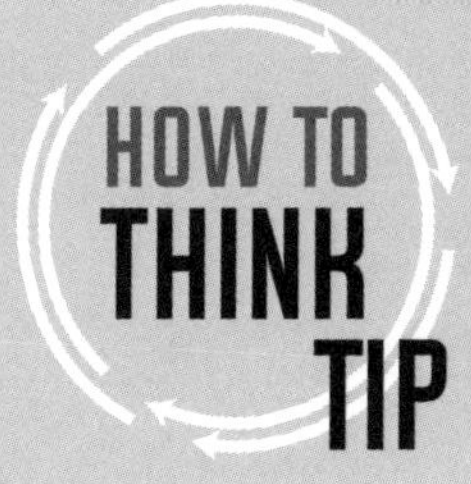

It may help you to know that you're allowed to repeat a number, although you mustn't go through the same square twice.

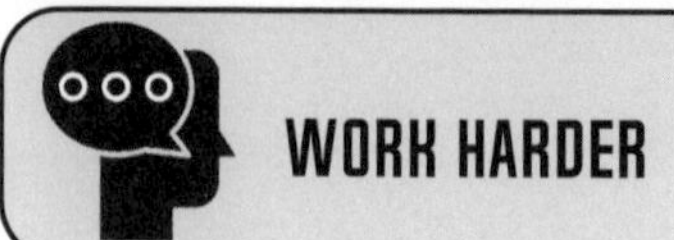

7-8 MINUTES

PUZZLE 45
NUMBERZONE 3

Practising decoding number sequences also hones your numerical logic. Artist Istvan has made a third Numberzone installation (see Puzzles 16 and 33), this time at an outdoor festival. Two tickets to the main stage are on offer to the person who can decide which of the five sets of numbers A–E to should be used for the fourth screen in the Numberzone. You have to identify the coded sequence Istvan sets up in the first three sets of nine numbers.

3	11	15
18	24	32
22	21	9

8	16	20
15	21	29
26	25	13

13	21	25
12	18	26
30	29	17

?

18	26	30
10	15	22
34	31	22

A

16	31	30
10	15	23
34	33	21

B

18	26	30
9	15	23
34	33	21

C

16	26	32
9	15	23
34	31	21

D

18	26	30
9	15	22
34	33	22

E

Look for a sequence involving individual numbers in matching positions in the first three squares. Number sequences are logic in action. For this reason, admirers of logic tend to enjoy making numerical calculations and unpicking number puzzles.

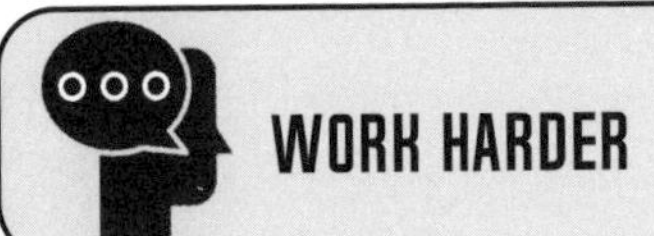

7-8 MINUTES

PUZZLE 46

SUDOKU 3

Stimulate your brain and build your numerical facility with this Sudoku (see also Puzzles 13 and 29). As before, fill in the empty squares so that each 3 x 3 block of nine, and each vertical and horizontal line, contains the numbers 1 to 9, once and once only.

4			1	2		9	3	
9	2							
1			5			2		
			3				6	
7	1						5	3
	8				4			
		1			3			2
							4	7
	9	7		6	2			5

The numbers in the four corners of the large square add up to 23.

PUZZLE 47

MASYU 2

Here's another chance to try your hand at a Japanese Masyu puzzle (see Puzzle 15). As before, your task is to draw a single continuous line around the grid that passes through all the circles. Here's a reminder of the rules: the line must enter and leave each box in the centre of one of its four sides; at a blue circle, the line must turn left or right; at a white circle, the line must pass straight through; the line must pass straight through the box before and the box after a blue circle without turning. The line must turn left or right in the box before and/or the box after a white circle. The line can turn left or right in an empty square. (Note that the line must not enter a box for a second time and must not cross over itself.)

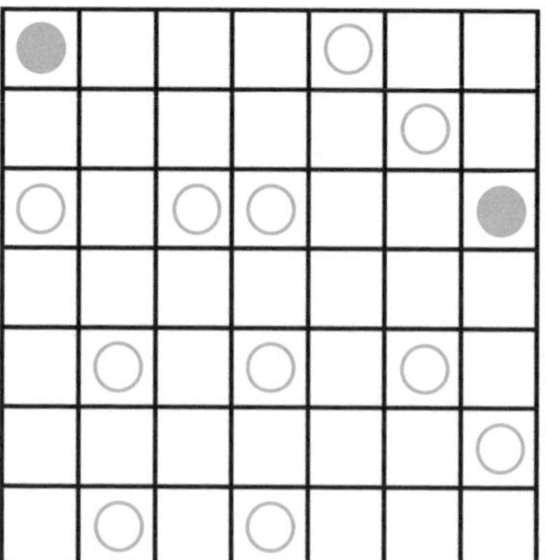

The starting point is not important here. You can start anywhere on the circuit, as long as you follow the rules laid out above.

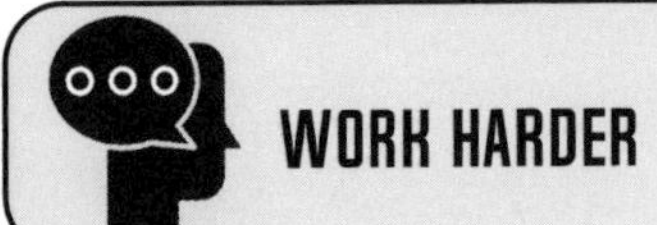

7-8 MINUTES

PUZZLE 48
NUMBER JIG 3

Before moving on to our Logical-Thinking Challenge, have another go at a Number Jig puzzle (see also Puzzles 11 and 30). As before, your task is to fit the numbers listed into the grid below. One five-digit number is provided to get you started, but choosing your next one may not be so simple. Which is a dead cert?

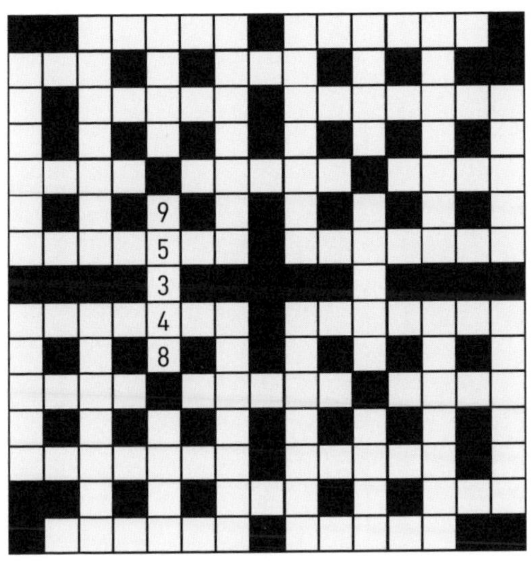

3 digits
158
175
238
245

4 digits
1698
3716
4189
4282
5230
6114
7024
8706

5 digits
16156
38752
38926
49240
50371
57853
76727
79263
93279
~~95348~~

6 digits
286348
615087
626325
672418

7 digits
1230427
1675846
2136618
2676920
3398117
3879154
4637613
5170954
5954256
6214155
6844231
7104518
8347528
8866178

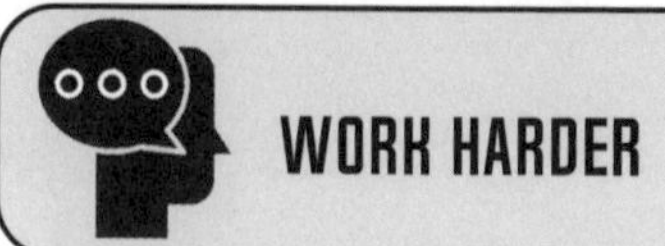

TIME PLUS

PUZZLE 49

NUMBERSEARCH 4

A numbersearch grid (see Puzzles 14, 27 and 32) gives you an opportunity to develop your skills in mental mathematics and numerical logic. As previously, your task is to make the calculations in the clues below, then find the answers in the grid in the way you would look for a word in a wordsearch puzzle. The answers in the grid may run backwards as well as forward, in either a horizontal, vertical or diagonal direction, but always in a straight, uninterrupted line.

1 83 + 78 + 278 + 8919
2 9874 + 391 + 84512
3 3982 + 3893
4 382 x 111
5 788951 + 43789
6 38903 – 38
7 34887 + 19900
8 388 x 38
9 93939 x 8943
10 85189 + 39438

8	7	1	7	5	1	8	7	1	3	5	9
5	7	7	4	6	9	0	0	4	8	8	1
5	3	7	8	9	0	7	5	8	4	2	1
5	8	8	3	2	7	4	0	6	1	5	9
7	8	4	1	9	0	5	7	4	8	4	1
5	7	4	8	7	1	0	7	5	7	8	2
5	2	1	5	2	8	4	1	7	1	9	3
5	8	0	8	6	4	3	7	1	7	5	8
5	8	5	4	4	5	8	3	2	7	7	2
3	3	8	9	2	3	1	7	8	5	0	3
9	7	3	8	1	4	0	7	5	8	3	1
7	8	1	3	5	8	6	3	9	8	7	1

Only one of the numbers runs vertically.

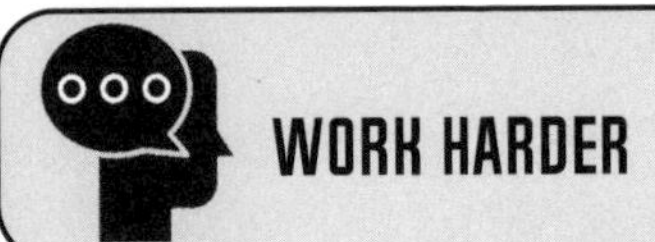

PUZZLE 50

SILENCE IN THE LIBRARY

In the faculty library, Robert and four other students are seated around the desk shown in the diagram below, all working very hard. Join them by studying these clues to discover the name and surname (one of which is Holt) of the student in each seat, together with the subject he or she is reading about. The following clues contain all the information you'll need to complete the information table. 1. The five students are Brian, the one reading a Biology book, the one surnamed Dart, the one (not Tina) reading a History book and the person in seat A. 2. The five students are Sue, the one reading a Chemistry book, the one surnamed Brown, the person in seat B and the person in seat E. 3. Sue (whose surname isn't Jones) isn't sitting directly next to Brian. 4. Four of the students are the one surnamed Fisher, the one reading an Art book, Louise and the person in seat D. 5. Four of the students are Louise, the one surnamed Jones, the one surnamed Brown (who isn't reading the Biology book) and the person in seat C. 6. Four of the students are Sue (whose surname isn't Fisher), the student in seat A, the one reading a Geography book and the one reading an Art book.

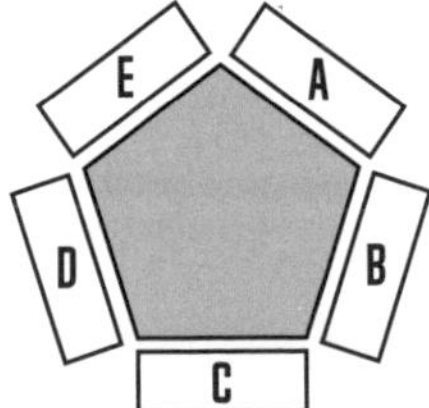

SEAT	NAME	SURNAME	SUBJECT

Take your time and use a scrap of paper or the Notes and Scribbles pages at the back of this book as you process the information.

THE CHALLENGE

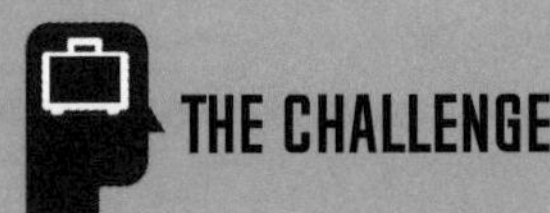

10-15 MINUTES

This final section of the book gives you the chance to put the logical-thinking skills you have developed into practice as you overcome challenges to your rationality in an almost-real setting. At this level of logical thinking, it can help to consider your thought processes as a string of lights like those on a Christmas tree. With these lights, when one bulb blows or one wire goes astray, the whole string stops working; you have to examine all the lights and connections, one at a time, to find thc problem. So check each step in your logic. Ask yourself: "How accurate is the premise? Does that step really follow from the previous one? Can I justifiably reach this conclusion?"

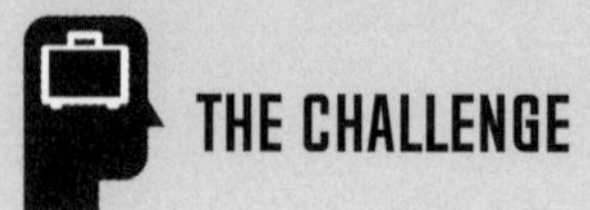

CAN LOGIC SAVE YOUR JOB?

The scenario that follows provides a test of your logical-thinking skills and a chance to try out strategies you have picked up in the course of the book. In this scenario you find yourself faced with a serious chain of problems at work first thing on a Monday morning – and because you are responsible and evidence appears to point at you, you urgently need to use logic in order to work out what has really happened and come up with a solution to defuse your boss's anger and deflect other possible consequences – such as losing your job!

Over the following pages, then, be ready to work hard in order to pin down the facts, to establish the inferences that you can draw from them and to plot a rational response. Maintain a degree of scepticism about what you are told. Interrogate what your problem seems to be and the communications you receive. Look beyond immediate appearances. Ask yourself, "Am I sure of what has happened? Can I see what is really being said?" When you think you know what has happened, draw up a plan to deal with the problems. Ask yourself, "How can I use logic to solve this issue by creating a simple sequence of steps that fits the evidence and leads from a justifiable premise to a rational conclusion?" Read the text through three or four times, noting down clues and ideas in the side columns provided. If you get stuck, remain patient. Keep trying to apply the simple rules of logic in order to sharpen your thinking.

THE CHALLENGE

10-15 MINUTES

You have a possibly disastrous start to the week at the small company where you work.

The background to your problems is this. The company, which devises puzzles and creates games, has six staff. Your boss, Ravi, is very creative but quite emotional. You are second-in-command and pride yourself on being clear-thinking and rational. There are also three designers – Alfie, Akin and Ana – and an IT guy named Moose. He is very quiet, but he gets thing done without advertising what he is doing. Although Ravi can be a handful, he is very warm-hearted – each day he sends an email to staff saying, "Good Morning Friends. Enjoy your work."

On Friday afternoon at 5 pm all the staff gather for a drink. Ravi makes a big fuss. First, his brand new laptop is not working properly – people are getting his emails days late and the messages are incomprehensible. Secondly, the locksmiths are very late in coming to fit a new security alarm and have just phoned to say they'll be there "some time this evening" – Ravi

NOTES & CLUES

10 -15 MINUTES

can't wait as he has a ticket for a concert. Thirdly, he has been promised a "yes or no" decision on a big contract, but the company in question, XYToys, won't decide until Monday, when Ravi is due to be in late.

"Don't worry", you say, "I'll stay to see the locksmiths. I'll deal with the contract. And I'll try to get your computer sorted."

Ravi acquiesces: "I'll send you an important email before I go", he says. "And I'll give XYToys your mobile phone number. Don't mess up this deal! The whole future of our company could depend on it – when you get the answer, be sure to respond at once!" Shortly afterwards, Alfie, Akin and Ana leave, followed by Ravi. "The laptop's on my desk", he says. Moose goes a little later, too, leaving you alone to deal with the locksmiths, who finally turn up at 8 pm. They set a new alarm, then show you how to use it. At 10 pm you lock up the office, set the alarm, then head home.
On Monday morning you reach your desk early. You log in to check your emails. There are two in nonsense English. Both are

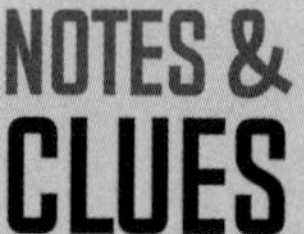

THE CHALLENGE

10-15 MINUTES

from Ravi. The first reads, "Fiis niebubf deuwbsa, Wbhit tiye qiej"; the second, "ZT qukk ewokt ub kwrrwe bynvwe xisw". "Oh dear". you think, "at least one of these is important".

Then you get a text from XYToys, but it is also incomprehensible. By now you're beginning to panic. Is there some kind of weird virus going round? How can it affect your phone? The text says, "2, 22, 8". What does that mean? You get a second text, saying, "14, 22, 22, 7–21, 12, 9–15, 6, 13, 24, 19–7, 12–8, 18, 20, 13–24, 12, 13, 7, 9, 26, 24, 7."

At this point you get an angry call from Ravi. "Just got in! Someone's stolen my laptop! We must have had a break-in! You set the alarm! Come to my office in 5 minutes – if you can't explain it, I'm calling the police!"

What do you do, or rather – how do you think?

NOTES & CLUES

THE ANSWERS

LOGICAL THINKING PUZZLES

Try to use this answers section as a source of inspiration. We all get stuck sometimes – we feel we're out of ideas and need help. If you're really stymied, it's fine to look up the answer to the problem. But after reading the solution, try to rehearse the steps in the logical-thinking process that led to the given answer, so you can adapt the strategy for future use, both with other puzzles in the book and in real life. As with all puzzles, it's possible that you may sometimes find an alternative solution – a sign that you're putting your logical brain to good use.

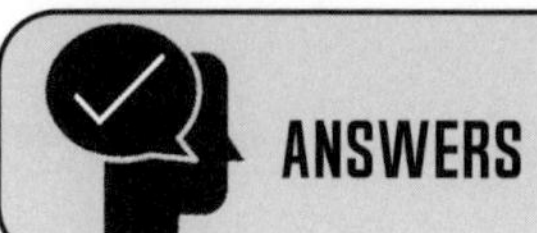

ANSWERS

PUZZLE 1
MR MOTHADA'S NUMBER PYRAMID

The missing numbers you needed to complete the pyramid are shown in the pyramid below. These puzzles quickly become addictive once you've worked out how to solve them.

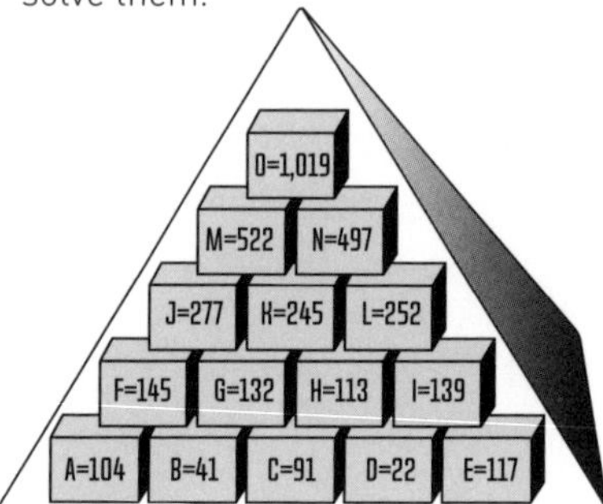

PUZZLE 2
NUMBER BOARDS

The missing numbers are 8 and 2, as shown below. Marcus works out that the odd numbers 1, 3, 5, 7 and 9 follow in sequence starting from the bottom left-hand square and increasing in a zigzag while the even numbers 10, 8, 6, 4 and 2 start in the top left-hand square and decrease in a zigzag.

10	3	6	7	2
1	8	5	4	9

PUZZLE 3
DREW'S DOMINO TABLE

The twenty-eight dominoes fit onto Drew's table as shown in the grid (right).

				4	5				
			3	4	1	6			
			4	3	6	4			
	3	3	0	5	0	6	2	6	
1	0	6	4	2	0	4	0	6	1
0	1	5	4	2	3	2	3	5	1
	3	5	1	2	2	6	0	0	
			1	3	1	4			
			5	6	5	5			
				2	2				

PUZZLE 4
COLLEGE BICYCLE BELLS

The History student lives in Saddle Street (Clue 1) and the Computing student in Handlebar Hill (Clue 4). The student in Wheel Way isn't studying Engineering or Psychology (3), so he or she must be studying Languages. Sharon lives in Chain Close (4). Jimmy, who is studying Engineering (3), lives in Bell Boulevard. Sharon is studying Psychology. Derek doesn't study History or Computing (2), so he must be the student in Wheel

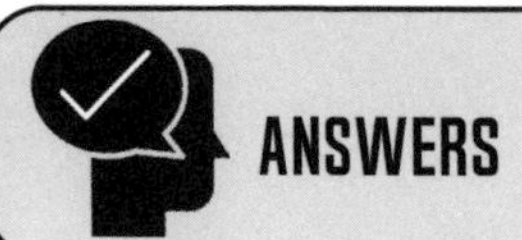

Way who is studying Languages. Hannah doesn't live in Saddle Street (1), so she must live in Handlebar Hill. Therefore George lives in Saddle Street. Derek has an orange bicycle (2). The silver bicycle isn't George's (1), Hannah's or Sharon's (4), so it must be Jimmy's. Sharon's bicycle isn't red or green (3), so it must be purple. George's bicycle isn't green (1), so it must be red. Hannah's bicycle is green.

Thus: Derek – Wheel Way – Languages – orange; George – Saddle Street – History – red; Hannah – Handlebar Hill – Computing – green; Jimmy – Bell Boulevard – Engineering – silver; Sharon – Chain Close – Psychology – purple.

PUZZLE 5
GRIDBLOCK

The completed grid is shown below. The Gridblock puzzles are marked "Time Plus" because they include the painstaking task of processing all the numerical clues.

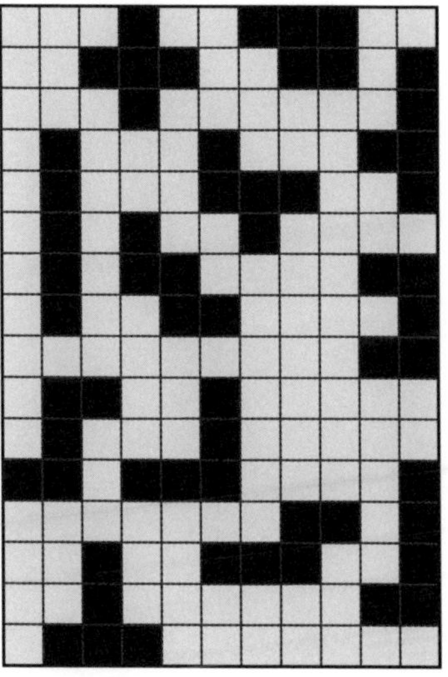

PUZZLE 6
"ONLY ONE OF THESE NOTES IS TRUTHFUL"

Perry's present is in the bread bin. The only truthful note is on the cupboard. If it had been in the fridge,the cupboard and bread bin notes would both have been truthful. If it had been in the

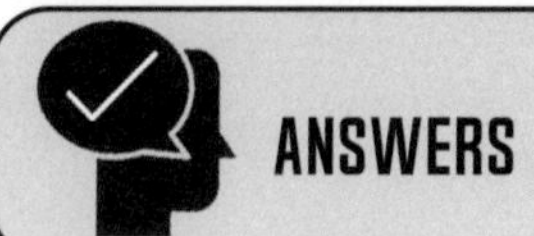

cupboard, the fridge and bread bin notes would both have been true. If it had been in the oven, the fridge, oven and bread bin notes would all have been true.

PUZZLE 7
THE "PATIENCE" OF HARRY STARRS

The cards total 84 (Intro), so there is no 7. Thus card F isn't a 10 (Clue 2). L isn't a 2 (clue 2). So the 2 of Spades is either I or K (Clue 1) and B, D, E, G, J and L are all Hearts or Diamonds (Intro). The value of card F is 3 higher than that of C (2), so the Ace of Hearts isn't B (3) or D, thus it's E or G. If G is the Ace of Hearts, then E is the 10 of Diamonds (1), I the 2 of Spades, K is a Club, and A is the 6. But then C is a 5 (2), F is an 8, and L is the Jack, leaving no value for B (4). Thus the Ace of Hearts is E (3), G is the 10 of Diamonds (1 and Intro), K is the 2 of Spades, and C is the 6 of Clubs. F is a 9 (2) and L a Queen. I is a Club, A a Spade, H a Club (3), and F a Spade. I isn't the Jack (4), so I is the 8 and H is the 5 (3). The Jack of Diamonds is D (4), B is the 4 of Hearts, L is a Heart, and J a Diamond. The King isn't A (2), so must be J. A is the 3.

Thus:	3S	4H	6C	JD
	AH	9S	10D	5C
	8C	KD	2S	QH

PUZZLE 8
CODE-CRACKING AT THE ZIGZAG

The new arrangement of books should be as shown below.

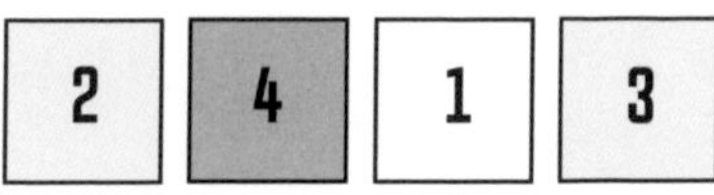

PUZZLE 9
TROPICAL FISH LIKE WARM WATER

The correct answer is F, as shown below. As Angus knew, you need to find the area of the diagram where the "yellow fins", "blue tails" and "glow in the dark" circles intersect without overlapping with the "cold water" circle.

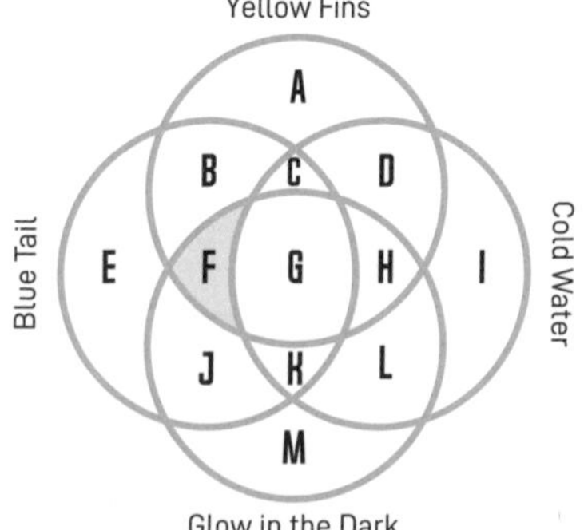

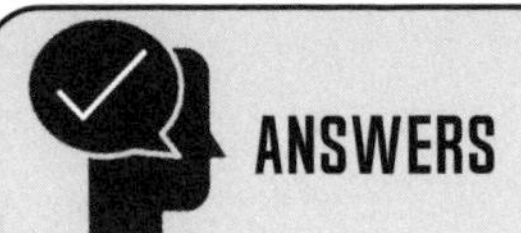

ANSWERS

PUZZLE 10
MAKE A SUM

With a little help from a client in the bar, Fabrizio arranges the coasters as shown below to make the sum 6 x 3 (=18) – 5 (=13) + 7 (=20) ÷ 4 (=5) + 8 (=13).

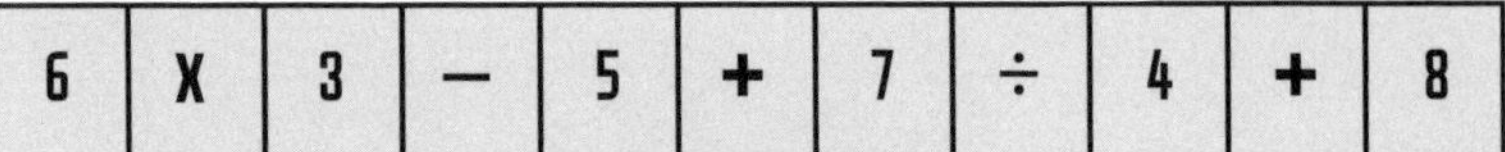

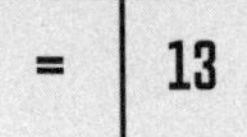

PUZZLE 11
NUMBER JIG

The completed grid is shown below. Puzzles like this are good for your numerical recognition skills and also hone your visual logic. You've done well if you completed it within the time limit.

		9	3	7	7	5		4	3	5	4	3	2	
1	8	7		0		6	5	2		2		4		
2		5	0	2	8	9		5	9	1	6	8	9	4
9		8		4		3		1		2		2		1
1	9	0	8		7	2	2	6	8		4	6	7	6
9		3		2		1		2		7		6		9
4	9	6	8	4	5	1		2	4	5	6	7	3	3
				0						9				
1	4	9	8	0	1	6		7	0	1	9	8	5	5
9		3		7		5		1		3		0		0
3	3	1	3		8	7	1	2	6		8	2	4	1
5		3		2		3		4		6		7		1
1	7	8	1	6	4	0		3	0	4	4	2		2
		5		0		7	6	5		0		9	6	3
	2	7	2	9	6	9		6	9	7	3	4		

PUZZLE 12
REBEKAH'S NUMBER WALK

The number walk drawn by Ethan was as shown below. After chalking it, he laid fluorescent rope along the lines to make a glow-in-the-dark design for the party.

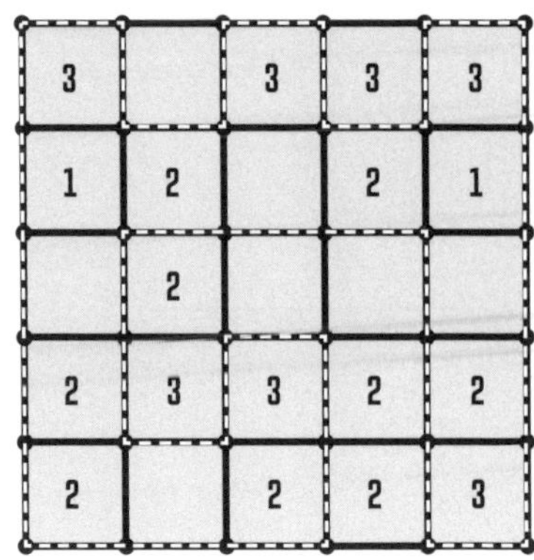

ANSWERS

PUZZLE 13
SUDOKU

The completed Sudoku grid is shown below. Sudoku puzzles are really good for developing logical thinking because you have to hold the list of possible solutions in your head and eliminate them one by one in a sequential fashion.

1	6	3	8	9	5	7	4	2
8	7	9	4	6	2	5	3	1
2	4	5	7	1	3	8	6	9
9	2	6	5	8	7	3	1	4
7	5	4	2	3	1	6	9	8
3	1	8	9	4	6	2	5	7
4	9	7	3	5	8	1	2	6
6	3	2	1	7	9	4	8	5
5	8	1	6	2	4	9	7	3

PUZZLE 14
NUMBERSEARCH

The answers you are looking for is 737531.

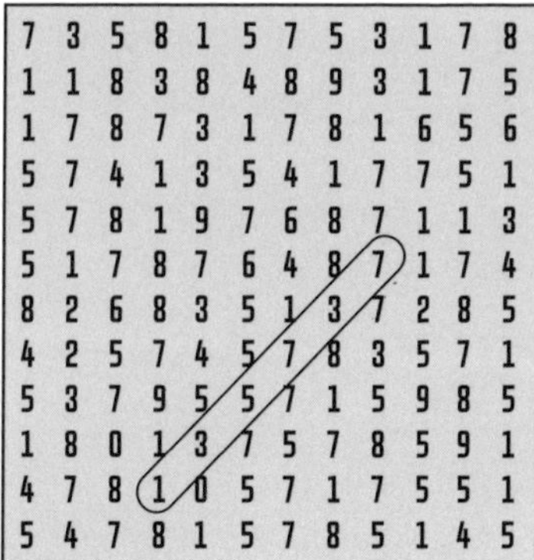

7	3	5	8	1	5	7	5	3	1	7	8
1	1	8	3	8	4	8	9	3	1	7	5
1	7	8	7	3	1	7	8	1	6	5	6
5	7	4	1	3	5	4	1	7	7	5	1
5	7	8	1	9	7	6	8	7	1	1	3
5	1	7	8	7	6	4	8	7	1	7	4
8	2	6	8	3	5	1	3	7	2	8	5
4	2	5	7	4	5	7	8	3	5	7	1
5	3	7	9	5	5	7	1	5	9	8	5
1	8	0	1	3	7	5	7	8	5	9	1
4	7	8	1	0	5	7	1	7	5	5	1
5	4	7	8	1	5	7	8	5	1	4	5

PUZZLE 15
NUMBERZONE

Akos chooses set B because he works out that in each of the three vertical columns of every set, the numbers total 13, 14 and 15.

6	4	7
4	5	2
3	5	6

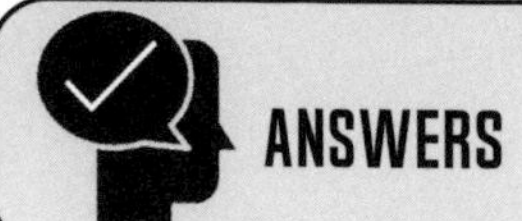

ANSWERS

PUZZLE 16
MASYU

The route through the completed Masyu is shown below. You'll see that the line always turns in the box before or after a white circle and that it always passes straight through the box before or after a box with a blue circle.

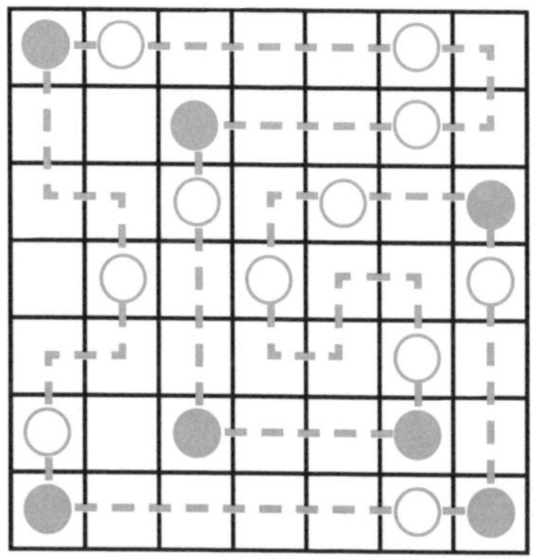

PUZZLE 17
CLYDE'S DOMINO TABLE

Clyde lays out the dominoes as shown below so the numbers on them match those painted on the table. He easily beats the time limit because he loves playing dominoes and is very familiar with the pieces and their combinations, and he also practises logic problems to keep his brain cells firing. Working out how things fit together in this way is good practice in simple step-by-step reasoning.

				4	6				
			5	2	6	6			
			4	0	3	5			
	2	5	4	4	0	5	4	0	
0	1	3	3	3	1	6	1	1	4
3	6	0	2	1	2	3	3	6	2
	0	6	1	4	1	0	0	5	
			1	5	2	6			
			3	4	5	5			
				2	2				

PUZZLE 18
FIVE FRIENDS AND THEIR PETS

Annie's dog is Captain (Clue 4). The girl with two fish isn't Josie (Clue 2) or Annie (4), so must be Caroline. William has six fish (3).

ANSWERS

So Michael is the boy with Rover (1), and has three fish, while Ginger lives with six fish (1). Josie has seven fish (2), so Annie has four. Joey and Spot aren't Josie's (2), so must belong to Caroline. Patch lives with six fish (5) and Sooty with seven, so Benjy lives with Sooty. Lenny belongs to Michael (5), so Bobby belongs to Annie.

Thus: Annie – Bobby – Captain – 4;
Caroline – Joey – Spot – 2;
Josie – Sooty – Benjy – 7;
Michael – Lenny – Rover – 3;
William – Ginger – Patch – 6.

PUZZLE 19
MIRROR SEQUENCE

The new sequence of mirrors is shown below. The star's movement of one square is to the right, with the square next to it, leaving the white shapes to occupy the two adjacent places to the left.

PUZZLE 20
NUMBER SEQUENCE BOARD

The missing numbers are 7, 12 and 14 as shown on the completed number board below. The numbers advance in sequence in an anti-clockwise spiral starting with 4. The sequence followed is + 2, then –1; so 4 (+2) 6 (–1) 5 (+2) 7 (–1) 6 (+2) 8 (–1) 7 (+2) 9, etc.

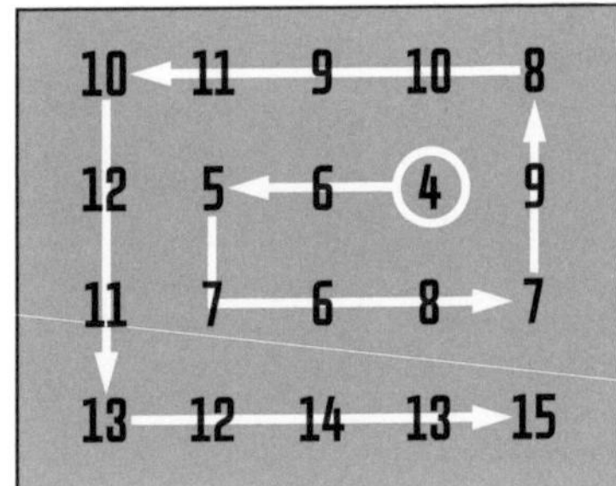

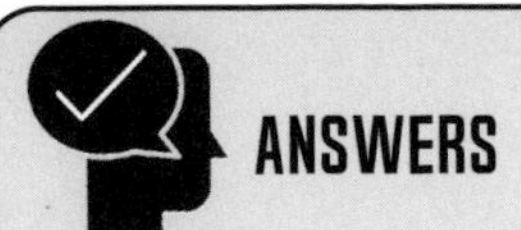

ANSWERS

PUZZLE 21
BICYCLE BELLS, BASKETS, LIGHTS AND GEARS

The answers are: 1. the section showing bicycles with bells and baskets but without lights or gears is B; 2. the section showing bicycles with lights but without bells or baskets or gears is I; 3. the section showing bicycles with bells and lights but without baskets or gears is D. Mr Alexis's bicycle belongs in section H.

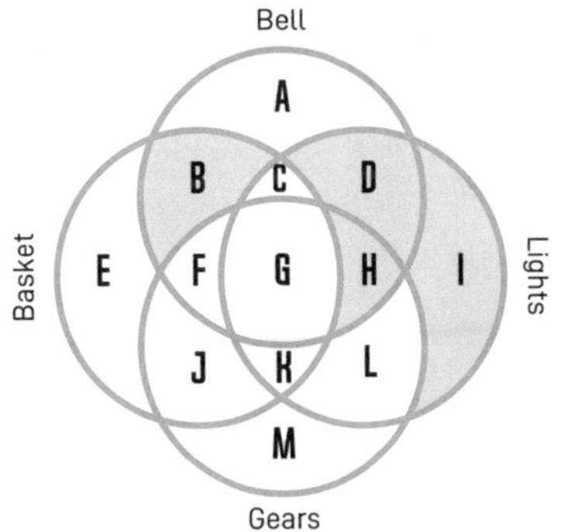

PUZZLE 23
ETHAN'S NUMBER WALK

The number walk drawn by Rebekah is as shown (right). As in other types of logical thinking, the key is to use reason consistently, step by step, following the simple rule that Rebekah devised.

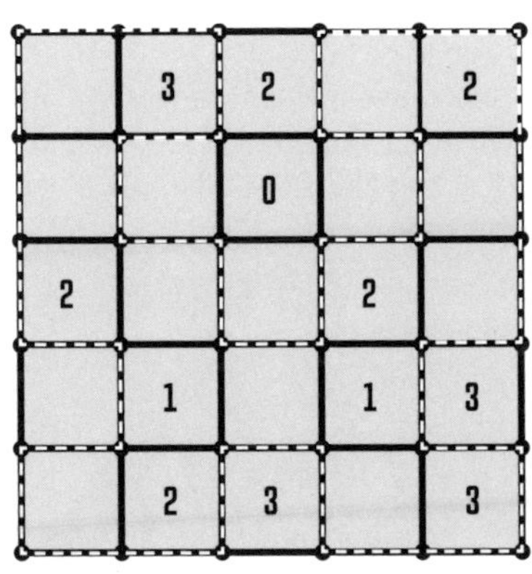

PUZZLE 22
MAKE A SUM 2

The sum that Angus makes is as shown below: 9 – 2 (=7) x 11 (=77) + 13 (=90) ÷ 6 (=15) x 3 (=45).

=	45

9	–	2	X	11	+	13	÷	6	X	3

PUZZLE 24
MR MOTHADA'S NUMBER PYRAMID 2

The missing numbers are shown in the completed number pyramid below. As suggested in the Tip on page 37, the best start is to calculate N (O [1,310] – M [587] = N [723]); then the third level down is an intriguing puzzle to track down three numbers that in two pairs add up to M (587[=266 + 321]) and N (723 [=321 + 402]).

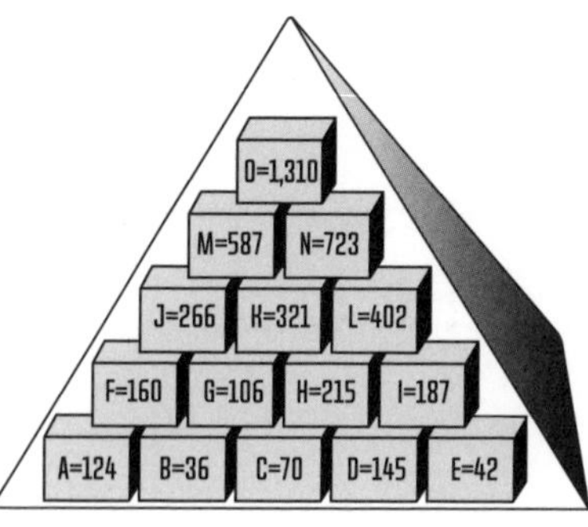

PUZZLE 25
GRIDBLOCK 2

The completed grid is shown below. As we've seen, developing visual reasoning is a key part of logical thinking. Some readers may find this kind of exercise quite a challenge, to others visual logic comes naturally and easily.

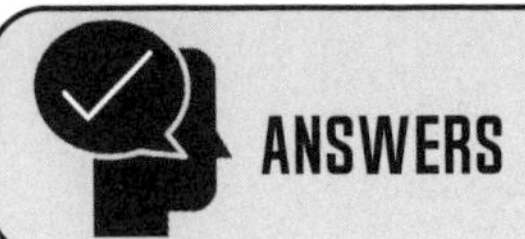

ANSWERS

PUZZLE 26
HARRY STARRS' SECOND STAKEOUT

The cards total 83 (Intro), so the 8 is missing. F isn't the 9 or Ace (Clue 4) and J isn't the King or 7; nor is F the 3 (Clues 2 and 4). If G is the 3, then K is the 9 (2) and J the Ace of Spades. But then B is a Club (intro), which leaves nowhere for the 5 of Diamonds (1). If C is the 5 of Diamonds, then G is the 7 (1), F is the King and K is a Heart (intro), which leaves nowhere for the Ace of Spades (2). Thus the Ace of Spades is either G or K (2), the 9 is H or L, and the 3 is D or H (2). Either way, H is either the 9 or 3. So B is the 5 of Diamonds, F the 7 (1) and E the King. J is the 6 of Hearts (4 and intro). L is a Diamond and D a Heart (intro). G is either a Heart or Diamond (intro), so the Ace of Spades is K (2), L is the 9 and H the 3. C and I are clubs and A is a Spade (intro). The 10 of Diamonds is G (3), C is the Queen and E is a Heart (intro). The 4 of Clubs (3) is I. The 2 is either a Spade or a Club (5), so is A, and H is a Spade, so F is a Club. D is the Jack.

Thus:				
	2S	5D	QC	JH
	KH	7C	10D	3S
	4C	6H	AS	9D

PUZZLE 27
NUMBERSEARCH 2

The answers are shown in the grid below. The numbers you are looking for are:

1 8956781
2 2901483
3 2313417
4 426217
5 410024182
6 931605399
7 1160
8 16380
9 10134
10 166320

4	3	3	3	7	8	4	3	1	0	1	4
3	2	5	8	7	3	3	8	7	3	2	2
2	1	6	7	3	1	8	9	3	9	9	2
3	4	8	2	3	2	8	4	9	3	2	2
3	0	5	8	1	0	7	3	1	5	1	8
7	8	8	3	2	7	5	6	3	0	9	1
5	3	7	3	1	0	0	5	3	9	9	4
3	5	6	8	6	5	1	0	7	3	2	2
5	6	3	1	3	1	1	5	1	1	6	0
1	2	3	1	3	4	1	7	6	4	9	0
3	9	8	9	7	4	5	8	3	9	0	1
5	3	8	1	8	7	6	5	9	8	9	4

PUZZLE 28
DEL'S DELIVERIES

Saturday's trip wasn't from Eastering (Clue 1), Southford (Clue 3) or Middleham (5), so either Northbrook or Westbury.The trip from Westbury was to Oneford (4). The one from Northbrook wasn't to Twobury (5), so the trip to Twobury wasn't on Saturday. No trips were

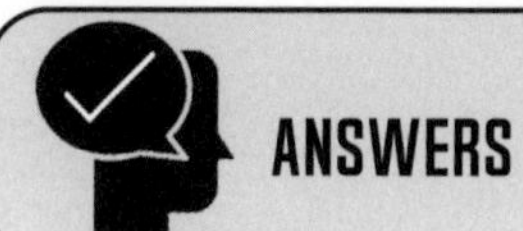

made on Wednesday (grid), so Tuesday's was from Middleham (5) and Thursday's to Twobury. Either the fruit was taken on Thursday and the trip to Foursham was on Friday (1), or the fruit was taken on Friday and the trip to Foursham was on Saturday: i.e. Friday's trip involved either fruit or a journey to Foursham. So the stationery was taken to Fivewood (4) on either Tuesday or Saturday and the Westbury–Oneford trip was on Monday or Friday. Thus Saturday's trip was from Northbrook. Monday's wasn't to Threeton (3) so must be Oneford. The stationery was taken on Tuesday (4). Thursday's trip was from Eastering (1), the fruit was taken on Friday and the trip to Foursham was on Saturday. Friday's trip was from Southford to Threeton. Saturday's delivery wasn't of cheese or shoes (2), so must be books. The cheese was taken on Monday (2) and the shoes on Thursday.

Thus: Monday – Westbury – Oneford – cheese;
Tuesday – Middleham – Fivewood – stationery;
Thursday – Eastering – Twobury – shoes;
Friday – Southford – Threeton – fruit;
Saturday – Northbrook – Foursham – books.

PUZZLE 29
SUDOKU 2

The completed Sudoku grid is shown below. Sudoku puzzles improve your general mental performance because juggling numbers and doing maths problems stimulates your brain to make cell connections, and this improves your efficiency, speed of thought and output in all areas of thinking.

6	2	7	1	8	4	3	5	9
8	9	5	3	7	6	4	1	2
4	1	3	9	2	5	8	7	6
3	5	9	7	4	1	2	6	8
1	8	4	5	6	2	9	3	7
2	7	6	8	9	3	1	4	5
5	6	1	2	3	8	7	9	4
9	3	2	4	5	7	6	8	1
7	4	8	6	1	9	5	2	3

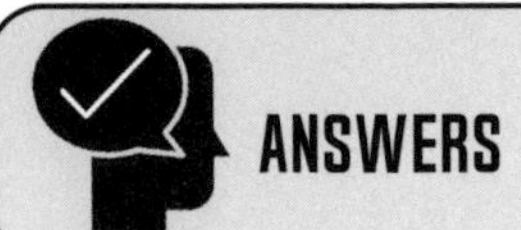

ANSWERS

PUZZLE 30
NUMBER JIG 2

The completed Number Jig grid is shown below.

		1	0	1	6	5		3	4	2	4	6	1	
4	3	3		5		2	9	8		8		3		
5		8	3	5	0	2		2	0	1	3	6	5	2
1		0		9		3		0		0		7		9
8	0	2	5		7	6	4	8	0		3	1	4	3
3		7		4		7		7		9		2		5
9	1	3	4	8	5	2		9	2	5	3	1	4	7
				5						7				
5	1	7	3	4	2	6		4	7	5	7	9	2	7
2		6		3		7		0		1		1		0
9	4	3	2		6	4	0	3	6		5	9	7	2
2		1		6		2		4		4		6		2
7	2	6	2	7	4	1		3	1	2	7	4		7
		2		0		8	2	2		9		1	1	6
	6	2	9	3	8	7		8	7	2	1	9		

PUZZLE 31
OPEYEMI'S BOOKCASE

The cookery book is small (Clue 2), so wasn't bought on Saturday (Clue 4). Saturday's purchase wasn't the thesaurus (1), atlas (2), the book on trees or the book on insects (3). Thus the weather book was bought on Saturday and is large (4), so (1) it's C and the thesaurus was bought two days before book B. The book bought on Friday isn't the thesaurus (above), atlas (2), and isn't on trees or insects (3), so it's the cookery book and the atlas was bought on Wednesday (2). The one bought on Thursday isn't the thesaurus (above) or on insects (3), so must be the book on trees. The atlas is large and was bought two days before the book on cookery (2), thus the atlas isn't B (1), so must be F. The book on insects was bought on either Monday or Tuesday, so isn't B (1). Thus B is the book on trees (1) and the thesaurus was bought on Tuesday. The insects book was bought on Monday. The cookery book isn't next to the atlas (2), so (3) the cookery book is D and that on insects is E. The thesaurus is book A.

Thus: Book A – thesaurus – Tuesday;
Book B – trees – Thursday;
Book C – weather – Saturday;
Book D – cookery – Friday;
Book E – insects – Monday;
Book F – atlas – Wednesday.

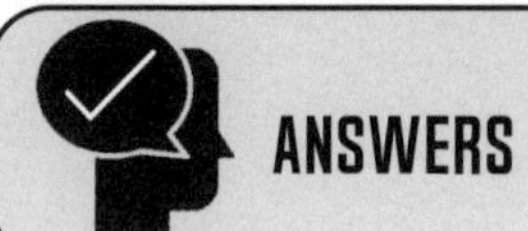

ANSWERS

PUZZLE 32
NUMBERSEARCH 3

The answers are shown below, followed by the grid.

1 81081
2 4903447
3 383322
4 138437
5 701296
6 44896663
7 19846
8 108864
9 45868200
10 86680

8	9	4	7	4	4	3	0	9	4	5	3
1	8	7	1	7	1	9	4	3	8	8	5
5	0	7	5	0	0	8	4	5	3	8	3
5	8	4	8	4	5	1	4	3	8	3	4
4	6	8	5	4	4	6	2	0	6	8	2
1	6	1	1	8	4	2	9	9	1	5	1
4	8	5	9	9	6	5	8	1	6	5	8
5	8	1	6	6	6	8	4	8	8	9	0
2	9	8	9	6	2	4	2	3	9	2	1
5	1	7	8	6	1	5	8	0	8	6	8
1	8	5	7	3	4	3	6	9	0	6	0
3	1	3	8	4	3	7	9	4	1	7	3

PUZZLE 33
NUMBERZONE 2

Gitta chooses set E because she works out that to match the sequence Istvan has created in the first three number blocks, she needs to find a set in which the numbers in the top and bottom rows are divisible by three, and those in the middle rows are divisible by seven. This is true of set E.

PUZZLE 34
VIKING LOGIC

Brunhilde takes one item, a skull, from the boxed marked "Mixed Goblets and Skulls". She then knows that because the box is wrongly labelled, the proper label must be "Skulls". As a result she knows that the box previously marked "Skulls" can't contain mixed goblets and skulls, because after swapping the labels, the "Goblets" label would be left on its original box, and she has been told that all three boxes have the wrong labels. So the old "Skulls" box must be full of goblets, and the old goblets box must be full of mixed goblets and skulls.

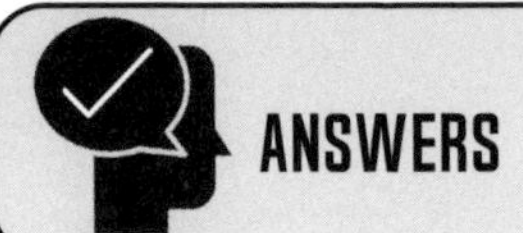

ANSWERS

PUZZLE 35
DECORATOR DOUGAL'S BUSY WEEK

Order: coffee shop, bank, crafts shop, florist, bakery, grocer's. The first shop on Dougal's list to paint is the crafts shop.

PUZZLE 36
HARRY STARRS' CARD STALL

The cards total 82, so the 9 is missing. The 10 is either A, B, C or D (clue 2), so the Queen isn't I or F (clue 3) and the 2 isn't F. Thus the Queen is either G, J or K (1), the 2 is H, K or L, and the 6 is D, G or H. So I isn't the 4 (3) of Clubs (2), which is thus either J, K or L (2). If the Queen of Diamonds is J, then K is the 2 (1), L is a Heart (Intro) and there's nowhere for the 4 of Clubs (2). If the Queen of Diamonds is G, then J and L are either Hearts or Diamonds (Intro), so the 4 of Clubs would be K (2), leaving nowhere for the 7. So the Queen of Diamonds is K (1), L is the 2 and H the 6. I and C are Hearts (Intro) and A is a Diamond. The 4 of Clubs is J and F is the 7 (2). B and L are Spades and D is a Club (Intro). I is the 5 (3) and the 6 is a Diamond (1), so F is a Heart (intro). E is either a Spade or a Club (Intro), so (4) the King is either a Heart or a Diamond. There's a card to the left of the King (4), so C is the King. E is a Spade and G a Club (4). A is the 10 (2), so (4) H is the Diamond with a value two lower than that of E, so E is the 8. The Jack of Spades is B, and D is the 3 (3). G is the Ace.

Thus:	10D	JS	KH	3C
	8S	7H	AC	6D
	5H	4C	QD	2S

PUZZLE 37
TIMEKEEPING TROUBLES

Lynne works in a shop (Clue 2). The woman who works in the library was 30 minutes late (Clue 2). She isn't Doreen or Erica (2) or Claire (4), so must be Marian. The woman with the faulty alarm clock wasn't 20 minutes late (4), so Claire was 50 minutes late and the woman who works in the theatre was 60 minutes late. The woman who is

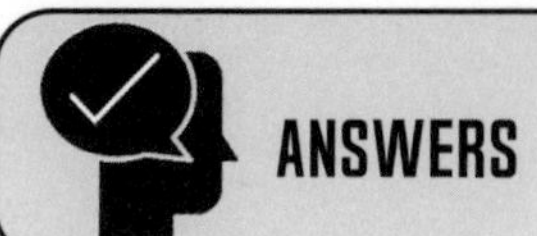

a teacher at the school was made late by the hailstorm (3). The woman who works in the theatre didn't have trouble with her alarm clock (4) and wasn't delayed by strong winds (3) or a fallen tree (5). Thus she was made late by black ice and (5) Claire was made late by the fallen tree. By elimination, Claire works in an office. The woman with the faulty alarm clock (4) was 30 minutes late (Marian, above), so Lynne was held up by strong winds. The schoolteacher was later than Lynne (3), so the schoolteacher was 40 minutes late and Lynne 20 minutes late. The schoolteacher isn't Erica (1), so must be Doreen. Erica works in the theatre.

Thus: Claire – office – fallen tree – 50 minutes;
Doreen – school – hailstorm – 40 minutes;
Erica – theatre – black ice – 60 minutes;
Lynne – shop – strong winds– 20 minutes;
Marian – library – alarm clock– 30 minutes.

PUZZLE 38
ANDRE'S VIRTUAL DOMINO TABLE

Andre's virtual domino table appears as shown below when complete. In Andre's video game called "Logick", players have to pass through several rooms containing tests of visual logic, verbal dexterity and clear reasoning before they can access higher levels at which they solve an involved puzzle of the kind presented in our Logical-Thinking Challenge (page 68).

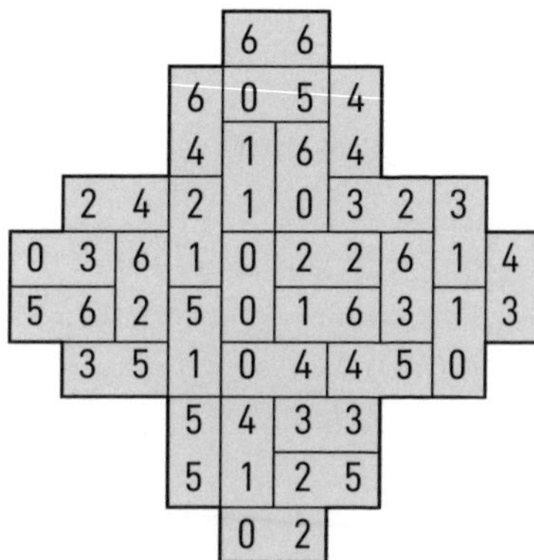

ANSWERS

PUZZLE 39
LETTER MATS

Andre arranges the mats in the Logica Hotel restaurant as shown below. A has not moved. Other variations are possible. Can you find them?

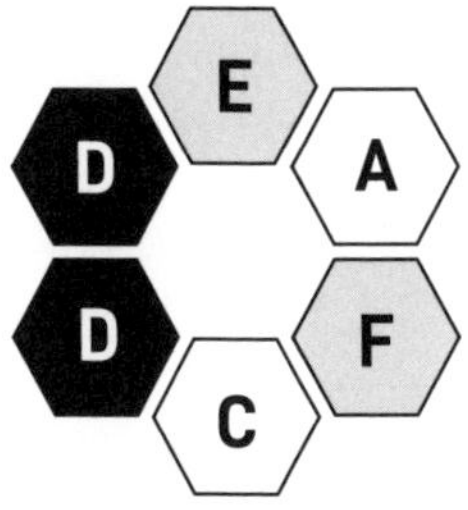

PUZZLE 40
JUMBLEHOURS

The missing numbers on Clarissa's jumbled-up clock are 15, 23 and 24. In each set of ascending numbers, the figures on the clock advance in seven-hour increments. So, 5, 12, 19, then back to 2, 9, etc.

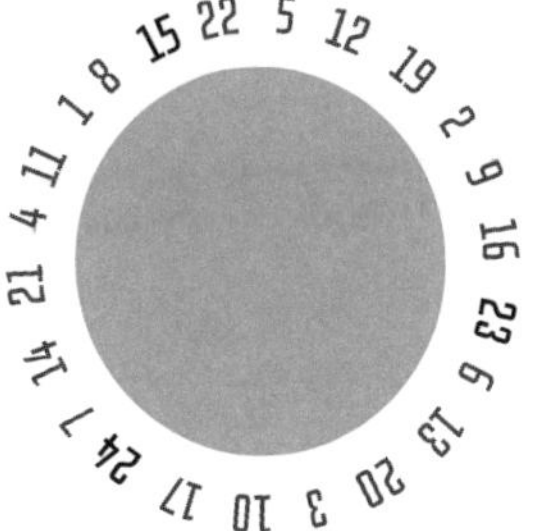

PUZZLE 41
CATS 'N' FISH 'N' FLEAS

The answers are 1. C; 2. L; 3. J; 4 B; 5. G; 6. H. They are highlighted below on a reproduction of Mr Alexis's Venn diagram.

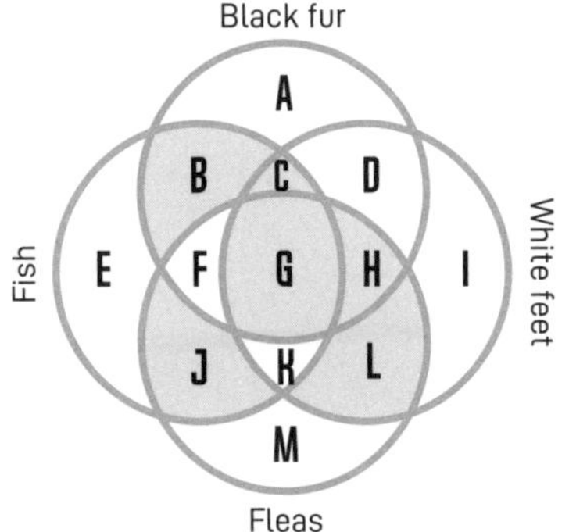

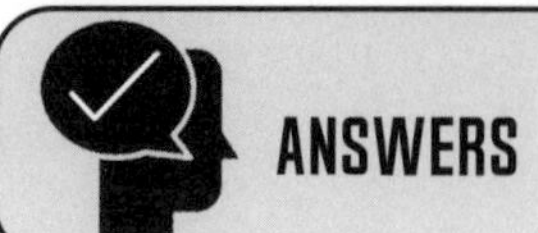

ANSWERS

PUZZLE 42
MAKE A SUM 3

The completed sum is as shown.
18+ 21 (= 39) ÷ 13 (= 3) x 32 (= 96) −11 (= 85) + 24 (=109).

18	+	21	÷	13	X	32	–	11	+	24	=	109

PUZZLE 43
GRIDBLOCK 3

The completed grid is shown below. By plotting information visually in this way, we are getting essential practice in the processes of logical thinking.

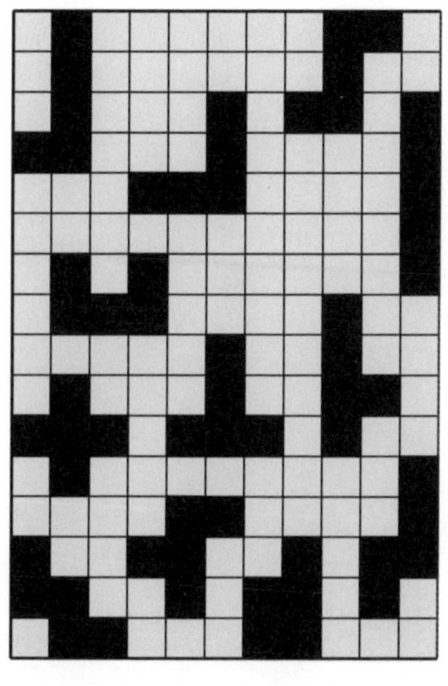

PUZZLE 44
PRIME NUMBER PATH

The path through the prime number room in Andre's video game is shown below. It passes the prime numbers 19, 37, 73, 79, 11, 2, 97, 89, 53, 5, 7, 71, 67, 23, 59, 31, 83, 23, 61, 79, 97, 17, 13, 47, 29, 59, 83, 19, 61, 2, 11 and 43.

4	30	68	63	49	27	9	19	87
18	22	14	89	97	2	15	37	81
17	44	66	53	4	11	79	73	9
29	12	77	5	24	49	77	33	57
71	23	36	7	25	59	31	83	23
16	45	18	71	67	23	62	15	61
2	61	19	14	8	18	44	12	79
11	10	83	59	29	47	13	17	97
43	62	99	21	32	33	46	75	55

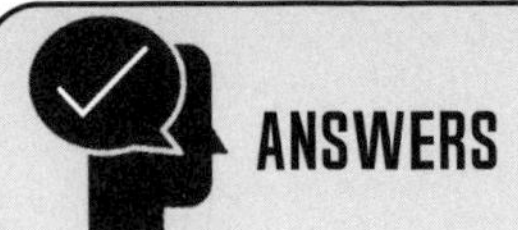

ANSWERS

PUZZLE 45
NUMBERZONE 3

The answer is C. To find the numbers in the left-hand column, add 5 to the top number in the previous box, deduct 3 from the middle number and add 4 to the bottom number. Then do the same for the other two columns. So you're looking for a square with left-hand column 18, 9, 34 and so on.

PUZZLE 46
SUDOKU 3

The completed Sudoku grid is shown below. Sudoku puzzles get our numerical and visual thinking working in tandem, and stimulate sharper mental performance.

4	7	5	1	2	8	9	3	6
9	2	3	6	4	7	5	8	1
1	6	8	5	3	9	2	7	4
2	5	4	3	9	1	7	6	8
7	1	9	2	8	6	4	5	3
3	8	6	7	5	4	1	2	9
5	4	1	8	7	3	6	9	2
6	3	2	9	1	5	8	4	7
8	9	7	4	6	2	3	1	5

PUZZLE 47
MASYU 2

The correct sequence is below. Just as in a good logical argument, each stage must lead to the next, according to the agreed rules.

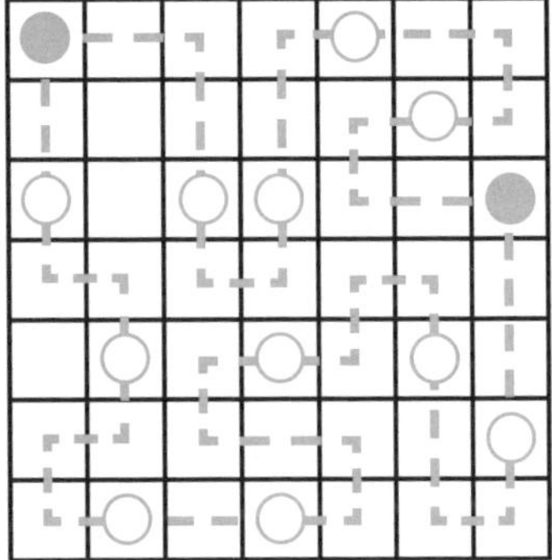

PUZZLE 48
NUMBER JIG 3

The completed Number Jig grid is shown below.

		3	8	7	5	2		6	1	5	0	8	7	
2	3	8		0		1	5	8		2		8		
8		7	9	2	6	3		4	6	3	7	6	1	3
6		9		4		6		4		0		6		8
3	7	1	6		7	6	7	2	7		4	1	8	9
4		5		9		1		3		5		7		2
8	3	4	7	5	2	8		1	6	7	5	8	4	6
				3						8				
1	2	3	0	4	2	7		5	9	5	4	2	5	6
6		3		8		1		1		3		6		2
1	6	9	8		5	0	3	7	1		8	7	0	6
5		8		6		4		0		4		6		3
6	2	1	4	1	5	5		9	3	2	7	9		2
		1		1		1	7	5		8		2	4	5
	6	7	2	4	1	8		4	9	2	4	0		

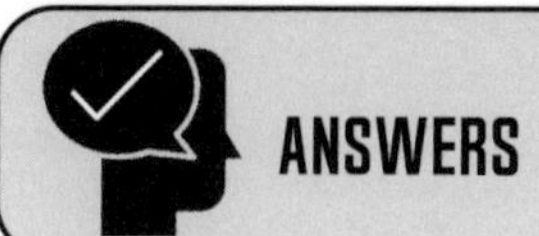

ANSWERS

PUZZLE 49
NUMBERSEARCH 4

The answers are:

1 9358
2 94777
3 7875
4 42402
5 832740
6 38865
7 54787
8 14744
9 840096477
10 124627

8	7	1	7	5	1	8	7	1	3	5	9
5	7	7	4	6	9	0	0	4	8	8	1
5	3	7	8	9	0	7	5	8	4	2	1
5	8	8	3	2	7	4	0	6	1	5	9
7	8	4	1	9	0	5	7	4	8	4	1
5	7	4	8	7	1	0	7	5	7	8	2
5	2	1	5	2	8	4	1	7	1	9	3
5	8	0	8	6	4	3	7	1	7	5	8
5	8	5	4	4	5	8	3	2	7	7	2
3	3	8	9	2	3	1	7	8	5	0	3
9	7	3	8	1	4	0	7	5	8	3	1
7	8	1	3	5	8	6	3	9	8	7	1

PUZZLE 50
SILENCE IN THE LIBRARY

The student in seat A hasn't a book on History or Biology (Clue 1), Geography or Art (Clue 6), so must be reading a Chemistry book. His/her surname isn't Brown (2). Nor is Brown in seats B, E (2) or C (5), so he/she must be in D. In clue 1, Brian and Mr/Ms Dart haven't books on History, Biology or Chemistry, so theirs are on Art and/or Geography. Thus Sue's surname isn't Dart (6). Nor is her surname Brown (2), Jones (3) or Fisher (6), so it must be Holt. Louise's surname isn't Fisher (4), Jones or Brown (5), so it must be Dart. Her book isn't on Art (4), so must be on Geography (above) and Brian's is on Art. Brian isn't surnamed Fisher (4) or (seat D) Brown, so must be Jones. The student in seat A isn't Sue (6) so is surnamed Fisher. The surname of the student with the Biology book isn't Brown (5), so must be Holt, and the one surnamed Brown has the History book and isn't Tina (1), so must be Robert. Tina's surname is Fisher. Sue isn't in seats B or E (2), so must be in C. Brian is thus in E (3) and Louise has seat B.

Thus: Seat A – Tina – Fisher – Chemistry;
Seat B – Louise – Dart – Geography;
Seat C – Sue – Holt – Biology;
Seat D – Robert – Brown – History;
Seat E – Brian – Jones – Art.

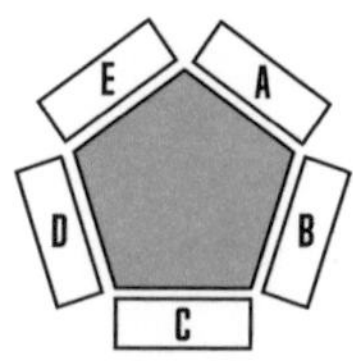

ANSWERS

THE CHALLENGE
CAN LOGIC SAVE YOUR JOB?

Ravi's emotional threats upset you for a few moments. And of course you doubt yourself, wondering whether you might have set the alarm wrong or left a window or door open when you locked up. Perhaps you are responsible for the missing laptop?

But then you decide to view the three things that have happened as challenges and, having calmed yourself with some deep breathing, you set about unpicking what clues you have.

You look at the emails from Ravi. You decide to work on the assumption that one of them is the normal email he has the machine set to send every morning. If this is true, you know what it should say. Suppose the machine is malfunctioning in a way that creates a code: "If I break the code", you think, "I can translate both his messages. One of them is the important message about XYToys. If I can translate that, perhaps I can make sense of their text messages."

You study his email, then look down at your keyboard. You see that the first word, which should be "Good" appears as Fiis. You see that I is just to the left of O on the keyboard. Could it be that the computer is misrouting letters so each letter in the email should be one further to the right?

You have it! The first message, "Fiis niebubf deuwbsa, Wbhit tiye qiej," translates (as it should) to "Good Morning Friends. Enjoy your work."The second is the one Ravi said was very important. It reads "ZT qukk ewokt ub kwrrwe bynvwe xisw." This translates as "XY will reply in letter number code."

A number code! Now you have the information you need to understand the text messages from XYToys. You decide to try the simplest letter number code you

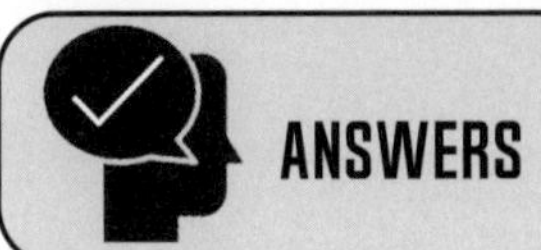

ANSWERS

can think of, in which each letter of the alphabet corresponds to a number, with A = 1, B = 2 and so on. This doesn't help much. The first text "2, 22, 8" translates as "BVH".

You don't give up. You keep plugging away. After a little trial and error, you try reversing that code, so that A = 26, B = 25 and so on. Now this looks promising. The first message translates as "Yes". The second one, 14, 22, 22, 7–21, 12, 9–15, 6, 13, 24, 19–7, 12–8, 18, 20, 13–24, 12, 13, 7, 9, 26, 24, 7, as "meet for lunch to sign contract".

Now you consider the missing laptop. You think of your training in logical thinking, and consider that if you have a false premise then the whole argument is wrong. In this case the premise is that the laptop is missing because it has been stolen. You decide to consider the possibility that it hasn't been stolen – where could it be? Is it anywhere in the office? You remember that all the staff were present when Ravi was complaining about his laptop, and recall that Moose has a reputation for acting without telling people. Suppose, you think, Moose simply took the laptop down to the IT department last thing on Friday? You email him to check.

By the time you go into Ravi's office you are able to tell him, "Don't worry. Everything's under control. I know where your laptop is and I've replied to XYToys. Are you free for lunch?"

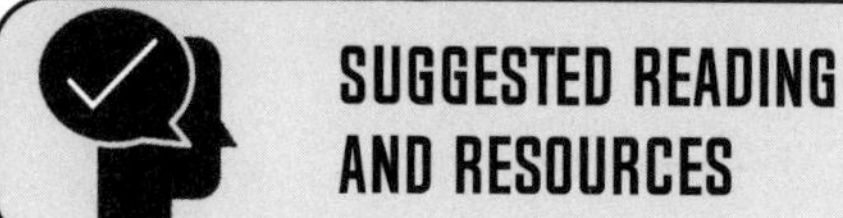

SUGGESTED READING AND RESOURCES

A Rulebook for Arguments by Anthony Weston, Hackett Publishing 2001

Asking the Right Questions: A Guide to Critical Thinking by Neil Browne and Stuart Keeley, Prentice Hall 2006

Being Logical: A Guide to Good Thinking by Dennis McInerny, Random House 2005

Brain Power: Learn to Improve Your Thinking Skills by Karl Albrecht, Prentice Hall & IBD 1993

Conquest of Mind by Eknath Easwaran, Nilgiri Press 2002

How to Win Every Argument: The Use and Abuse of Logic by Madsen Pirie, Continuum International Publishing Group 2007

Logic: A Very Short Introduction by Graham Priest, Oxford Paperbacks 2000

Logic Book by Charles Phillips, Metro Books 2008

Logic for Dummies by Mark Zegarelli, John Wiley & Sons 2006

Make the Most of Your Mind by Tony Buzan, Pan Books 1988

My Best Mathematical and Logic Puzzles by Martin Gardner, Dover 1994

Practical Intelligence: The Art and Science of Common Sense by Karl Albrecht, Jossey-Bass 2007

Shortcut by David Macaulay, Dorling Kindersley 1995

Straight and Crooked Thinking by Robert Thouless, Pan Books 1974

"The Red-Headed League" in *The Adventures of Sherlock Holmes* by Sir Arthur Conan Doyle, Penguin Classics 1994

Teach Yourself: Training Your Brain by Terry Horne and Simon Wootton, Hodder Headline 2007

The Dhammapada Translated by Eknath Easwaran, Nilgiri 2007

Thinking from A to Z by Nigel Warburton, Routledge 2007

Websites:
www.puzzlechoice.com
www.gameminds.com
www.rinkworks.com/
www.logicgamesonline.com

THE AUTHOR

Charles Phillips is the author of 20 books and a contributor to more than 25 others, including *The Reader's Digest Compendium of Puzzles & Brain Teasers* (2001). Charles has investigated Indian theories of intelligence and consciousness in *Ancient Civilizations* (2005), probed the brain's dreaming mechanism in *My Dream Journal* (2003), and examined how we perceive and respond to colour in his *Colour for Life* (2004). He is also a keen collector of games and puzzles.